Slogging
Toward
The
Millennium

Pulitzer Publishing Company
900 N. Tucker Blvd.
St. Louis, MO 63101

Book production by Debra Clark, Mark Bernard, Cindi Crismon Anderson
Edited by Marie Holdener and Cindi Crismon Anderson
Cover Design and Illustrations by Dan Martin
Printing by Kingery Printing Company

McClellan, Bill, 1997.
Slogging Toward The Millennium / Bill McClellan
p. cm.

ISBN 0-9661397-1-2 Perfect Bound
ISBN 0-9661397-0-4 Case Bound
I. Title. II. Title: Slogging Toward The Millenium.

Printed in the United States of America
1 2 3 4 5   KPC   6 7 8 9 10

II

Bill
McClellan

Slogging
Toward
The
Millennium

CONTENTS

FOREWARD

On a wintry night in January of 1983, while serving as night police reporter for the St. Louis Post-Dispatch, I stopped by Rena's Den in south St. Louis. With its dancing girls and its bawdy atmosphere, it resembled a saloon in a frontier town. In fact, Rena herself reminded me of a raunchy version of Kitty from "Gunsmoke."

Considering the late hours of my visit, it all seemed appropriate. As night police reporter, I had come to the conclusion that the frontier was no longer a place, but a time. The later the hour, the farther away from civilization.

How very romantic it seemed to work the frontier beat.

On this particular night, I was doing just that. I was checking out a police report I had read the night before. There had been an arrest at Rena's.

Rena herself told me the incident had not taken place in the bar, but in a van outside the bar. Not much to it, she assured me.

A young man — wearing a cowboy hat! — overheard our conversation, and mentioned an arrest of his own. A bad arrest, he said. Rena must have been in a one-upsmanship mood, because she then dragged out a newspaper story about a time she had been arrested for lewd and lascivious behavior. The article was from The Evening Whirl, and had been written by Ben Thomas.

Ben Thomas, my friend and rival. If ever there was a frontier character, it was Ben. He would have been writing pulp fiction in the Old West, immortalizing the gunslingers and the marshals. In fact, that's exactly what he was doing in 1982. In his newspaper, the homicide detectives were "killer-catchers" and "H-Men," and the narcotics detectives were "N-Men," and everybody had nicknames. The detectives were Dapper Dan, George the Creeper, Steve the Smasher and Jerry the Huntsman. The bad guys were saddled with names like Skunk and Dope-Eater.

Compared to the stuff I wrote, which was always heavily laced with the word "allegedly,'" Ben's prose rang with truth.

It was as if we were both writing about the Frankie and Johnnie shooting. "They allegedly had an argument, and then she allegedly shot him," I'd write, while Ben would turn out a blues song that would be remembered forever.

Perhaps his real forte was the way in which he wrote about crimes as if had seen them. "I try to imagine the way it probably happened," he once told me, "and then I write about what I saw."

Which was, incidentally, the way he had written the story about Rena. It was a very descriptive story about her being lewd and lascivious. Rena liked it enough to save it because he had called her a 46-year-old go-go dancer with the body of a 30-year-old. I should also mention that Rena denied she had been lewd and lascivious in this particular case, and she had eventually beaten the rap. One story that made the rounds at police headquarters was that she had really been lewd and obnoxious, but because there was no statute covering obnoxious, they had thrown the lascivious charge at her. Maybe the people who were selling that story believed that a woman can't be lascivious if she's over 40. But even then, when I was under 40 myself, I didn't subscribe to that theory.

But that is neither here nor there. This is not supposed to be about Rena or Ben. Instead, it is supposed to be a foreword to a collection of columns.

Because what happened shortly after that night was this: I was called back from the frontier and assigned a job as columnist.

It was even more fun than being night police reporter. I no longer had to sprinkle the word "allegedly" throughout my stories. As a columnist, I was allowed to express my opinion. I have now been expressing my opinion for 14 years. I have been allowed to do so throughout a number of changes at the newspaper. Editors have come and gone. Managing editors have come and gone. City editors have come and gone. Sometimes I feel like a cat that hangs around an apartment. The new residents may like the cat, or they may dislike the cat, but they continue to feed it.

So it has gone with me.

Now I have been asked to put together a collection of columns. I thought it would be an easy task, and that the reader of such a collection would come away with at least a superficial understanding of St. Louis. I was wrong on both counts.

Selecting the columns has been painful. Rather, not selecting certain columns has been painful. For instance, how could I omit the story about the Irish wake that Judge Evelyn Baker had for her late husband at a downtown saloon? As the pallbearers carried the coffin into the saloon, the judge said to me, "This is the first time he's ever been carried into a place like this."

But omit it I did. Along with a number of other columns that I liked. Oh well.

This is also not, it turns out, any kind of representative look at St. Louis. A reader of this book will not learn that the place to buy pizza dough is the Missouri Baking Company, and that Lino Gambaro, the patriarch of the bakery, would ask a novice pizza-maker (as he once asked me) if he drinks, and if the novice were to answer in the affirmative (as I certainly did) that Leno would explain that the secret to a good crust is to let the dough rise for two beers.

Nor will the reader learn that our most celebrated political record — akin to Joe Dimaggio's 56-game hitting streak — belongs to former alderman Sorkis Webbe Jr. He was sworn in as an alderman at an 11 a.m. and a grand jury, that very day, returned an indictment against him at 1 p.m. Shortest elapsed time between induction and indictment. Two hours.

It was, actually, a blessing. Right away, the other aldermen knew that Webbe was a regular guy.

I could go on and on about what this collection of columns is not.

What it is, though, is a hodgepodge of stuff I have written in the last 14 years.

In an effort to give this collection some semblance of form, I have separated the columns into four categories. The first has to do with the criminal justice system, of which I know something from my days on the frontier. The second has to do with my own misadventures as I stumble forward with other Baby Boomers toward middle age and the Millennium. A third has to do with women and business and politics. These three fit together easily because I understand so little about any of them. The final chapter deals with everything that didn't fit into the first three.

All of the columns appear exactly as they appeared in the newspaper, with one exception. I have changed the names in one column. That's the column about the male law student who bit a female law student. I changed the biter's name because I believe there ought to be a statute of limitations for jerkdom. Maybe the guy is reformed. I hope so. I changed the victim's name because even though she did nothing wrong, the matter was a source of some embarrassment to her.

As a final note, I would like to say that if I had been writing a column during my days on the frontier, I would have championed Rena's cause. I still think she should have been convicted.

I

Crime and Punishment

A Buried Past Tugs at Detective's Heart

The letter from Florida was addressed to the circuit attorney in St. Louis. It found its way to Tom Murphy's desk in the homicide unit on Monday morning.

"I am enclosing a copy of my husband's birth certificate. We are trying to get information about his parents," the letter began. "When he was real small, before he could remember, his parents committed a robbery. His father was killed and his mother probably did prison time."

The letter-writer said that her husband had been raised by relatives. She said he had heard various stories about his parents' problems.

"Could you please help us find out just what did happen? Then perhaps he can let it go," the letter-writer said.

Murphy read the letter, took note of the the pleading quality at the end, and then looked at the birth certificate. James Leo Mitchell was born on June 11, 1929. The birth certificate indicated that the birth had been at home, not at a hospital. The mother was 16. The father was 23.

At first glance, Murphy does not seem a sentimental person. For 30 years, he was a city cop, and for 25 of those years, he was a detective. Although he is now the chief investigator for the circuit attorney, he still wears a fedora, the mark of an old-school detective. His world is a rough place.

But something about the letter touched him. He thought about the man, now 64, searching for his past. He thought of the man as a child. What kind of stories had the child been told?

Murphy supervises a staff of 24. He could have assigned somebody else to look into the case. Instead, he picked up the phone and called the Mercantile Library.

"I had the father's name from the birth certificate, and I figured that if he had been shot during a robbery, it would have made the papers," he said. "Since Mitchell was too young to remember any of it, it had to have happened between 1929 and 1934."

Sure enough. The librarian found something on microfilm.

Four days before Christmas in 1930, Leo Mitchell was shot while trying to rob a card game.

Newspapers were colorful in those days, if not entirely reliable. In one account, Mitchell was carrying a sawed-off shotgun. In another, he was carrying an automatic pistol.

By all accounts, the shooting took place in a saloon — this was, remember, during Prohibition — and the man who shot Mitchell was an off-duty cop named Fred Hollman.

One of the newspaper accounts described the shooting:

"Mitchell ordered the men in the place to 'stick em up.' Hollman raised his left hand, whipped out his revolver with his right hand and opened fire." Mitchell was hit twice, but managed to run outside, where his wife was waiting in a cab. Later, he died at City Hospital. His wife was arrested.

Knowing the date of the incident, Murphy was able to find the old police records. He even found the mugshot of Mitchell's wife.

Mary Christine Mitchell was a hard-looking young woman, staring defiantly toward the camera. The police report indicates she was as hard as she looked. Except for denying knowledge of the robbery attempt, she refused to answer questions.

The report also said she was released the next day. So what happened to her?

"Unfortunately, they didn't have Social Security numbers in those days, and that makes it hard to track somebody down. Also, I had two different dates of birth — one from the birth certificate of her son, the other from the police report after her arrest," Murphy said.

He called the archives section of the Missouri Department of Corrections, but they couldn't locate anything.

Murphy did find out, however, that Leo Mitchell was on parole at the time of his attempted robbery. He had done five years of a 10-year sentence for second-degree murder.

Within a couple of days, Murphy had a thick folder together. Newspaper accounts, police reports, court records. He even went to the scene of the robbery and shooting —it's still a saloon — and took photographs. He located the apartment where Leo Mitchell and his wife lived in 1930 and took photographs.

"I'm going to give the guy a first-class job," Murphy told me Wednesday afternoon. "He's going to know that somebody cared about this."

The only thing Murphy didn't have was information on Mary Christine Mitchell.

"I'm going to have to call the guy and get the names of some relatives. I just need a little more information, and then I'll be able to track her down,"Murphy said.

There was no phone number mentioned in the letter, so Murphy tried information. No listing. He called the local cops in Florida, gave them the address and asked them to tell James Leo Mitchell to call him. Tell him he can call collect, said Murphy.

Thursday morning, Murphy got a call from James Leo Mitchell's wife.

Thanks for your help, she said, but it's too late. My husband killed himself. He was buried on Tuesday.

For a long time after he hung up the phone, Murphy sat at his desk. Then he sighed, and picked up a new file.

Sunday, October 31, 1993.

A Loser Gets His Day in Court

Charley Lucas went to court Friday in Hillsboro.

The prosecutor was recommending that Judge John Anderson revoke Lucas' probation. That would mean that Lucas would go to prison to serve a five-year sentence for selling marijuana. I wrote about the case last week.

Nine years ago, Lucas took $40 from two undercover cops and used that $40 to buy the cops a little less than an ounce of pot. He made no money on the sale. Nevertheless, he was among those indicted when the undercover operation came to a close.

Except for a minor traffic ticket, Lucas has not been in trouble since.

His problem largely has been one of money.

When he was first arrested in 1983, he couldn't raise $2,000 for bond, so he was thrown into the Jefferson County Jail.

Months later, his case went to court. He was placed on three years' probation and ordered to pay court costs. Included in those costs was more than $2,000 for room and board in jail.

Lucas didn't pay, so the county revoked his probation. Lucas couldn't make bond, so he went back to jail.

By the time he got to court, his bill was more than $5,000. The judge extended his probation, and Lucas was released.

But he didn't pay any of his $5,000, and he missed a few meetings with his probation officer. So last month, he was arrested again.

"Charley Lucas is one of life's losers," I wrote.

I noted that he had dropped out of high school. I

noted that he didn't have a great work record. When he was arrested last month, he was living with a cousin and working off his rent by working in her video store.

"It doesn't seem fair to put a guy in prison because he can't afford to pay for being in jail, when he wouldn't have gone to jail in the first place if he could have afforded bond," I wrote.

Shortly before court Friday, I chatted with Lucas' cousin, who said that, yes, her cousin sure was one of life's losers. She recalled how excited he was when, as a kid, he got a bicycle.

Then he took his bike for a spin — freedom! — got hit by a car and spent a year in a body cast.

The revocation hearing began on a good note for Lucas. Public defender Larry Schmidt argued that Lucas had been sentenced to three years of probation more than six years ago and therefore, for some legal reason, the court could not revoke his probation.

I didn't understand the legality involved, and I'd be willing to bet that Lucas didn't. But the prosecutor, chief trial attorney John Appelbaum, leaped to his feet and pointed a finger at poor Lucas.

"When it comes to interpreting this statute, the defendant wants it both ways!" he said.

Then Lucas' probation officer testified. She said that Lucas had missed several meetings. She said he had moved from his mother's house to his cousin's house a block away without notifying her.

Under cross-examination, she testified that if Lucas had been able to make his bond the first time, his court costs would have been less than $100.

Then Lucas testified. He said that when he was working at his cousin's video store, he made $30 to

$50 a week. He said he spent the money on his girl-friend.

"What would you have the court know about your failure to pay?" Schmidt asked.

"I really don't have the money. That's the truth of it," Lucas said.

Appelbaum was fierce in cross-examination.

He brought up the fact that Lucas smokes cigarettes, and he suggested that if Lucas quit smoking, he could pay the county the $5,000 he owed for spending so much time in jail.

Then he got into the matter of Lucas squandering 30 bucks a week on dates.

"Did you ever suggest to your girlfriend that you stay home and watch a movie?" he asked.

Finally, Appelbaum brought up the fact that Lucas has spent the last seven years on probation or in jail.

"Isn't it a fact that you've done nothing but ma-nipulate the system?" he asked.

Then the judge took over.

"I'm not like Mr. McClellan," the judge said to Lucas. "I don't like to say that another human being is a loser.

"But even if you're King of the Losers, you still have to pay rent," the judge said.

"We want to give this young man the full benefit of the law," the judge said, as he announced that he would render a decision in about 10 days.

As the deputies led Lucas back to jail — a place he literally cannot afford to be — I thought he looked more like a loser than like a guy manipulating the sys-tem.

Sunday, April 8, 1990.

Policeman Becomes His Brother's Keeper

Circuit Court Judge John Riley had been through this before. A young defendant stood in front of the bench with his public defender at his side. The kid was pleading guilty to assault and armed criminal action.

The state was recommending 10 years. The kid and his lawyer indicated they were ready to accept the deal.

As a matter of course, though, the judge asked if the victim had anything to say.

Dmitri A. Cole stood up. He's a city cop.

It was a little more than 17 months ago that he was shot. He was having some work done on a rental house he owns, and he thought he'd drive over and see how the work was going. He always carries his service revolver — his wife sometimes complains about that habit — but on this day, July 10, 1995, he started to pick it up, and then he thought, "Oh, I'm only going to be gone for a minute."

He got into his 1992 Mazda. He pulled up to a stop sign in the 5500 block of Cote Brilliante.

Willie Williams was sitting on a porch with two friends as the Mazda eased toward the stop sign. Williams was 15. He had a .22 revolver. He decided — if you can call a spur of the moment thought a decision — to get the car. He approached the passenger side of the car. He hollered something. Cole looked up and saw the glint of metal in Williams' hand. Instinctively, Cole threw his right arm up. A bullet crashed through the glass and into his arm. He stepped on the gas and drove away.

Williams was arrested shortly thereafter. He was certified to stand trial as an adult.

The assault charge carries a sentence of five to 15 years, and armed criminal action carries three to life.

The state offered 20 years. Because of the truth-in-sentencing statute for violent crimes, Williams would have to serve 85 percent of the time. He would spend 17 years in prison.

His public defender, Rich Moran, came up with a counteroffer. My guy will plead to 10, he said.

The prosecutor called Cole. What do you think of 10? he asked. I'll consider it if I can meet the guy, Cole said. So last month, Cole went to the Workhouse to meet the young man who shot him.

"Why'd you shoot me?" Cole asked.

"I dunno," said Williams.

Both Cole and Williams are black, but in a way, they come from different planets. Although Cole's mom and dad divorced when he was young, he and his two brothers and two sisters were raised in a loving, middle-class home. He joined the Marine Corps after graduating from high school. After a four-year hitch and a stint as a security guard, he joined the police department. He always wanted to be a cop. He is 31 years old.

Williams, on the other hand, spent most of his youth in a boys' home in Texas. His mother is in prison. He never knew his father. He came to St. Louis to live with his aunt.

"I want to tell you how lucky you are," Cole said to his assailant. "If I would have had my gun, I would have killed you. I would have felt bad about it because I didn't join the Police Department to kill kids, but I would have done it."

Williams never looked Cole in the eye, and he couldn't explain why he had shot him —he had no juvenile record and was doing all right in school —

but he didn't try to come on like a tough guy, and that in itself made an impression on Cole.

"You've got to go to prison," the cop finally said. "You've got to be punished. But I'm going to go along with the 10-year recommendation, and while you're in there, I want you to stay in touch with me. When you get out, I'll try to help you."

Later, Cole talked the whole thing over with his wife and his family, and everybody thought he was doing a good and righteous thing. Then he told his barber, Bobby Bennifield, who cuts hair and dispenses philosophy at the House of Grooming in the 3700 block of Page.

"If you give him 10, you might as well give him 20," said Bennifield. "He'll be gone, anyway."

And so it came to pass that on Tuesday morning, Cole stood up in front of Judge Riley and began to speak.

Cole recommended that the sentence be halved. Five years was enough, he said. He explained that he knew that Williams should go to prison, but with a shorter sentence there was a better chance of salvaging a life.

"As a police officer, and also as a black man, I think it's my job when it comes to a case such as this for me to go beyond what, you know, an average citizen might do. Because if we don't help him out now, he'll get out and do the same thing again possibly," Cole said.

The judge was stunned. He turned to the defendant.

"You're just incredibly fortunate that your victim was somebody who cares about you for whatever reason," the judge said, and then he went along with the cop's recommendation, and sentenced Williams to five years.

A couple of days later, Cole reflected on what he had done. He said he definitely intended to stay in touch with Williams.

"I don't want to ask for leniency, and then forget about it, and be responsible for him getting out and doing it again," Cole said. "You know, I was reluctant to do this because of my job. I don't want to be seen as being soft on crime, but then again, this was not a professional thing. It was a personal thing."

Friday, December 20, 1996.

Lawyer Closes Estate Work with a Will

Unlike so many people, Marguerite Crain had a real fondness for lawyers. At least, there is some indication that that's true — she left a large chunk of her estate to her lawyer, despite the fact that he billed her unmercifully in the last years of her life — and even if it weren't true, it would be nice to think so.

Otherwise, she is surely turning over in her grave. A flock of lawyers in the St. Louis County Courthouse is currently hovering over her estate case. In 1983, when Crain, who never married, had her will prepared, everything seemed simple. She left her entire estate, which today is valued at more than $3 million, to her cousins. She was 80 years old at the time.

But in later years, she changed her mind. First, she created a trust and named her lawyer, James L. Sullivan, trustee. Then, in 1986, she made a new will, which transferred most of her estate to the trust controlled by Sullivan. In 1987, in a codicil to her new will, she left the family home to Sullivan. She also spent $366,000 to rehab the family home, and turn it into a law office. In 1989, shortly before she died, she left the rest of her property to Sullivan.

Not that he was doing too badly even before her death. When she sold some property for $3.5 million, Sullivan received a fee of $396,000.

Furthermore, at the time of her death, he was charging her a monthly retainer of $3,000. In addition, he took her to his country club for lunch every Friday, and charged her $250 for his time.

In fairness to Sullivan, there did seem to be some kind of estate-planning going on. That is, his estate. In the event of his death, his son, Christopher Sullivan, was to become the new trustee.

After her death in 1989, when her relatives learned the terms of her new will, several of the cousins sued. According to their lawsuit, Crain was suffering from senile dementia in the last years of her life and was unduly influenced by her attorney.

As per law, the cousins had to sue all the beneficiaries of the new will, which included, oddly enough, the Humane Society. Seldom do you find a person broad-minded enough to love both lawyers and dogs.

Jury selection began Monday, and the courtroom seemed crowded with lawyers. There were, of course, the lawyers representing the cousins who were suing, and there were lawyers representing the Sullivans, and the trust, and the cousins who weren't suing. There was even a lawyer representing the Humane Society.

In addition, the court appointed a lawyer to represent minor children and unborn children who might be affected by the terms of the will. Whether this lawyer represents the unborn children of the cousins, or the unborn children of the Sullivans, was unclear.

As the various lawyers questioned the potential jurors, only the lawyer for the dogs was brief. Was there anybody who hated dogs? Or cats? Was there anybody who felt that a person shouldn't be able to leave some money to a charity?

The other lawyers had a more difficult time, especially the defense lawyers.

"Just because a lawyer is named in a lawsuit to overturn a will, would you start with the presumption that there's some merit in the lawsuit?" is the question that Sullivan's lawyer asked.

That was, I thought, a clever way of asking the really key question: Was there anybody on the panel who hated lawyers?

After all, the linchpin of the whole case is clearly going to involve the state of mind of the deceased. Was she mentally alert, as the defense claims, or was she suffering from some kind of dementia, as the plaintiffs claim?

Judging from the terms of her new will, she liked lawyers.

Obviously, then, the defense would have to find 12 citizens willing to consider the premise that a person with a sound mind could like lawyers.

In *voir dire*, one potential juror admitted that she had been involved in a contested will case.

"Could you give my client a fair trial?" asked Sullivan's lawyer.

"No way!" said the potential juror.

Eventually, however, by Tuesday at noon, 12 jurors and two alternates were selected.

Opening statements were about what you'd expect. The lawyer for the cousins painted Sullivan as a greedy, manipulative swindler. The lawyer for Sullivan painted the cousins as greedy, uncaring relatives, and painted his client as a very fine attorney who rendered faithful legal services to the deceased.

I left before the lawyers for the unborn children and the dogs gave their statements.

But I'll be back. There are two very intriguing witnesses. They each specialize in something called "legal ethics."

I have to find out what the heck that is.

Wednesday, June 3, 1992.

Law and Justice: Yin against Yang

Judge Henry Autry sat in his chambers one morning last week. He was eating a carton of low-fat yogurt and smoking a cigarette.

The yin and the yang, I thought. He understands the yin and the yang. In a perfect world, all judges would have that understanding, but in the real world, judges are only lawyers with political connections.

So it's heartening to find a judge who understands that wisdom requires a sense of balance.

For just as health has its yin and yang, so does the legal system. You have the law, and you have justice. Only occasionally do the two come together.

Consider Holmes v. Smith, a case Judge Autry presided over earlier this month. He has yet to announce his decision.

James Holmes married Judy Smith in 1973. Three years later, Smith got a down payment together and Holmes used his VA benefits to buy a house.

Smith and her children moved into that house. Holmes continued living with a woman who Smith thought was his aunt.

Smith and her children made all the house payments. They paid all the taxes. They did all the repairs.

When Smith and Holmes broke up in 1980 — there was never a divorce — Smith and her children continued making the payments, paying the taxes and keeping the house in good repair.

Earlier this year, Holmes and his wife, the woman Smith had always believed to be his aunt, sought to evict Smith and her children from the house.

The trial was like an episode of "Night Court."

Holmes was a reluctant witness.

"Are you married to my client?" Smith's attorney asked.

"I'm married to Mattie," Holmes answered, referring to the woman Smith once thought to be her husband's aunt, but who, it turns out, had been his wife since 1946.

Finally, Judge Autry interceded, and insisted that Holmes give a direct answer.

Yes, I'm married to Smith, too, said Holmes.

Smith was a theatrical witness.

She responded to questions the way a terrier responds to a rat. She attacked. She attacked from all directions at once and did not allow herself to be limited by a specific question. One thought led to another.

Holmes' attorney, who had read a column I had written earlier about the case, demanded to know if Smith had ever been jailed for welfare fraud.

Certainly not! she said indignantly. It was a conspiracy to commit fraud charge that got her, but anyway, even while she was in jail, the mortgage was paid by her children, and not by Holmes.

Holmes' original wife was an evasive witness.

She said she didn't know much about anything, that her husband took care of all the family business.

"Isn't it true that your husband can't read?" Smith's attorney asked.

"I don't know about that," said Holmes' wife.

Again, the judge interceded. "You've been married to the man, and have lived with him since 1946, and you don't know whether or not he can read?" the judge asked.

"It's never come up," said the wife.

And so it went. What a bizarre trial.

I was left with the distinct impression that the law is

on Holmes' side. The deed is in his name, so if he wants to evict a person living in his house, then legally, he ought to be allowed to do so.

Yet justice seems to be on the side of Smith. She's paid for the house, and she's lived in the house. Besides, when Holmes signed for it, Smith thought she was his wife, which she was — sort of.

If my wife wanted a car, but I signed for it because I'm the one who belongs to the credit union, and then she made the payments, wouldn't it be considered her car if our marriage broke up?

But Smith and Holmes can't divorce because technically they were never married. You can't marry a woman when you're already married.

So it falls upon Judge Autry to sort the whole thing out.

When I visited him several days after the trial, I asked when he would make his decision.

Soon, he said.

Then he ate a spoonful of yogurt, and took a drag from his cigarette.

I think he was working himself into the right frame of mind to weigh the yin against the yang.

Sunday, August 20, 1989.

Many Ifs and Ands Concerning a Bite

John Smith, looking like a misunderstood preppie, sat on the witness stand Wednesday, and admitted that yes, he had bitten Jane Jones on her rump.

At the time of the biting, Smith was a third-year law student at St. Louis University. He had spent his undergrad years at Vanderbilt University. He had prepped at John Burroughs. Thousands and thousands of dollars worth of education had come down to this. He was being sued for biting a young woman on her rump.

At the time of the biting, Jones was a law student at Washington University.

Both Jones and Smith are now practicing attorneys.

Jones' attorney, Gerry Greiman, was questioning Smith about the night in September 1987 when Smith spotted Jones in a crowded bar and decided to bite her.

According to testimony, she was enraged.

"Did you tell her that she should take what you did as a compliment?" Greiman asked.

"I believe I told her that," Smith said.

It's always hard to read juries, but I stared intently at the 12 St. Louisans who were hearing this case. They looked like normal, everyday people, which was appropriate, because it would be up to them to determine the community standards.

Should a woman be flattered, or offended, if a man she's never met bites her on the rump?

After all, that was really the question. There was no question that Smith bit Jones, and bit her hard enough that she went to a doctor. Then she sued. She was asking for "reasonable" damages.

"When you bit Miss Jones, this was not the first

time you've bitten a woman on the buttocks without her consent, was it?" Jones's lawyer asked.

"No, it wasn't," admitted Smith.

It turns out he had bitten at least two other young women without their consent, but in fairness to Smith, these bitings occurred several years ago, when he was in undergraduate school.

He stared into his past and tried to recall the incidents.

The last one's name was Stephanie, he said. He added that he couldn't recall her last name. The one before that, he couldn't remember her name at all.

Obviously, Smith is not a young man who pays attention to a woman's name. He's more interested in other aspects of a woman's, uh, persona.

"Did you ever bite any other women on their buttocks without their consent?" Jones's lawyer inquired.

"I believe it might be possible," Smith said.

Then Smith's lawyer, David Hoven, took over.

"Were you angry with Miss Jones when you bit her?" he asked.

"No," said Smith. "I didn't intend to hurt her."

Under the friendly questioning of his lawyer, Smith explained that biting a strange woman on her buttocks is, well, it's a way to get to know her.

Stephanie, for instance. The one whose last name he couldn't recall. He later dated her, he said.

Well, who knows? Maybe this is the kind of behavior a young man learns at expensive private schools.

Certainly, it seemed acceptable to Smith.

That feeling was reinforced Wednesday afternoon, when the lawyers read a deposition to the jury. The deposition had been given earlier by one of Smith's pals, who was with him the night he bit Jones.

The friend recalled that Smith spotted Jones across the room.

"Somebody should go bite her on the butt," Smith supposedly commented.

I suppose it's cheaper than buying her a drink.

But I shouldn't make light of this. Jones suffered a great deal of pain — she couldn't sit down for three days — as well as humiliation and embarrassment.

Her attorney mentioned all this in closing arguments Thursday morning.

Greiman suggested that $25,000 would compensate Jones for her suffering, and an additional $25,000 would punish Smith for his behavior.

"Women ought to be able to go into public places without fear of something like this happening," Greiman said.

Then it was Smith's turn, and he wisely avoided defending his client's behavior.

"John did something foolish. He shouldn't have done it," Hoven said. Then he argued that whatever humiliation and embarrassment Jones had suffered was being compounded by a public trial. This trial is Jones' idea, he said.

Hoven also argued that Jones was a successful young lawyer, so the humiliation and embarrassment had not caused her career to suffer.

Meanwhile, Smith sat impassively at the defense table.

You might not be what you eat, I thought, but in this instance, you are what you bite.

Friday, April 20, 1990.

Private Fantasies in a Public Court

As Dewey Crump's drug trial resumes this morning, the state representative will again be forced to sit in a federal courtroom and try to act dignified.

But if things keep going the way they've been going, the legislator's dignity will take another beating. To truly appreciate the whole spectacle, you have to understand something that court-watchers learned last week.

Crump is a 43-year-old teenager.

With that in mind, imagine this: Somebody has secretly taped the goofy stuff you said when you were 18 years old, and now those tapes are being played in an open courtroom. What's more, people are pretending that you said that stuff recently!

Last week, Crump sat in the courtroom and listened to himself boast about the time he watched a pal and a woman have sex on his boat.

Everything is sex. He bought his boat because women can't resist a guy with a boat. Even the drugs that have put Crump in the courtroom had to do with sex. When former state representative Bob Feigenbaum wanted to lure Crump into getting cocaine, he baited the hook with women. I know a couple of girls who want drugs, Feigenbaum said.

For Crump, whose brain is located somewhere below his belt, that was enough. We'll give them Dr. Dewey's dosage, he chirped happily.

Sex, sex, sex.

Of course, we men are complicated machines. Our physical side is constantly fighting our intellectual side. With most of us, it's a constant struggle. The yin and the yang.

With Crump, the yin has happily surrendered. He's a yang guy.

"I want to get naked and crazy!" he proclaimed on one of the tapes that was played last week.

It was during jury selection that I first caught a whiff of the way things were going to go.

One of the prospective jurors admitted that he was on probation for indecent exposure. The government's attorneys pleaded with the judge to dismiss the prospective juror from the panel.

We don't want a guy like this on the jury, they said.

Crump's lawyers argued that the man would be a fine juror.

I looked at Crump, sitting quietly at the defense table, and I thought, "It's come to this. The legislator is hoping for a jury of perverts."

Unfortunately for Crump, the flasher didn't become a juror.

When the flasher was dismissed, I thought, "So much for a jury of your peers."

Only a flasher could understand a guy whose goal in life is to get naked and crazy.

Crump might have more trouble with everyday guys.

Frankly, Crump is the kind of guy that most of us didn't like in high school. He's big and nice-looking and self-confident, the kind of guy who always did well with girls.

Those of us who weren't big and nice-looking and self-confident would look at Crump and think, "He's shallow. Why do all the pretty girls think he's so cool?"

Now, years later, here he is, King Cool, 43 years old going on 19, sitting at the defense table, and the nerds are nipping at his heels.

The assistant U.S. attorneys who are prosecuting him look like guys who couldn't get dates to the prom.

Feigenbaum, the government's star witness, ranks even lower on the cool meter.

Worse yet, the men on the jury look like everyday guys. Perhaps they're thinking about the Crumps they knew in high school, especially when they listen to Crump blabber away on the tapes about sex, sex, sex.

If you think he's got an advantage with the women on the jury, you're probably wrong.

Although he likes women — that's an understatement! — he doesn't seem to respect them. At least he doesn't sound too respectful when he chatters away about them on the tapes.

Sex, sex, sex.

As I said, his brain seems to be located somewhere below his belt.

Even as this fact has become painfully obvious, Crump has done his best to act dignified.

During the breaks, he chats with the reporters, another bunch of guys not scoring too high on the cool meter.

Here is one thing he has said to several of us: "If I wasn't innocent, I wouldn't be here."

I suppose he means that if he weren't innocent, he wouldn't be suffering the indignity of a trial. But still, it sounds strange the way he says it.

Last week, one of the television reporters asked him about the embarrassing tapes.

If you listen to those tapes and you think you understand this whole story, Crump said, it's like you read 10 pages of "War and Peace" and you think you understand the whole book.

Perhaps he has a point.

But I wish he wouldn't have used "War and Peace." Something a little raunchier would have been more appropriate.

Maybe "Dewey Does Dallas."

Monday, September 10, 1990.

A Law's Legality is in the Eyes of the Beholder

T he only political prisoner in St. Louis County was led into the courtroom Friday morning. He was handcuffed. The handcuffs, incidentally, were not removed during his court appearance.

He was wearing his gray jailhouse uniform. In the best of times, Bruce Kurt was tall and thin, but 10 months in the county jail had left him positively gaunt. With a wispy beard and a manic glint in his eyes, he looked like a mad artist.

The court clerk, Ed Fitzgerald, a man who loves Jack London and personally knows the beat poet Lawrence Ferlinghetti, and has, not surprisingly, more or less befriended the county's only political prisoner, walked up to Kurt.

"Don't get upset," said Fitzgerald.

"Get upset?" replied Kurt.

He was already upset. He always gets upset when he goes to court. In fact, I first wrote about him when he wore deer antlers to court to show his disrespect for the system. Courthouse regulars still refer to Kurt as Bullwinkle.

He was in his glory when he was wearing those deer antlers!

"You're a biased son of a bitch," he told the judge that day. The judge, who had pointedly ignored his antlers, ignored his outburst. "You're a perfidious son of a bitch," Kurt said, and the judge sentenced him to 10 days in jail.

"If I have to look the word up, he goes to jail," the judge told me later.

He was in court back then on the very charge for which he is now serving time — driving on a suspended or revoked license. He was eventually convicted and sentenced to a year.

He was back in court Friday for a hearing on another charge involving the same offense. For that matter, there is a warrant pending against him in Douglas County for the same offense.

Part of the problem comes from the fact that Kurt does not believe the government has the right to require a citizen who is not engaged in commercial traffic to have a drivers license. He bases this argument on a statute passed by the first Congress in 1789 that declared that citizens be allowed "unhampered use of all navigable water and all common law highways."

But still, uncharacteristically, he once gave in to his principles and got a drivers license. Then he got a ticket for speeding on a motorcycle in Nebraska in 1987. When he refused to pay the fine, Missouri suspended his license.

Kurt decided that this was unconstitutional — Congress had not authorized the interstate compact under which his license was suspended — and he argued his case all the way to the Missouri Supreme Court. He lost.

That was no surprise to Kurt. He believes that judges are illegally seated and that lawyers are illegally licensed.

At any rate, he was in court Friday morning for a hearing about yet another case of driving on a revoked or suspended license. His chief argument seemed to be that the warrant was illegal because it said he had failed to appear and he said he had never been notified to appear.

As Fitzgerald later pointed out, that's a pretty good argument, if only because Kurt is not a failure-to-appear type. He seems to enjoy the combat. In fact, he seems to feel that it is his duty to confront the illegal judges in their illegal courtrooms.

He made that clear when he addressed Associate

Circuit Judge Carolyn Whittington after he had argued that the warrant was illegal.

"I do not waive my contention, by speaking here, that the International Bar Association is a foreign government," he said.

Whittington seemed to take his declaration in stride. She gazed down from the bench at Kurt, who stood there, handcuffed and defiant, obviously intelligent in the way that all mad artists are obviously intelligent.

Perhaps realizing that this was a man who did not really belong in jail — we're letting real criminals out because of overcrowding — the judge said she was going to issue a recognizance bond on the case in front of her. A recog bond means no money need be posted. The defendant is released on his word alone that he will appear for trial.

Because Kurt has served almost a year on the charge for which he was given a year, a recognizance bond would mean his imminent release.

"I won't sign anything!" he shouted.

The judge shrugged, and the bailiffs led Kurt out of the courtroom.

Later that day, he called me at the newspaper.

"I might be getting out today," he said.

But that would depend, I knew, on several things. Would Douglas County exercise its warrant on him? Would he consent to sign the recog bond, and if he didn't, what would happen then?

This much I know. If he gets out, he doesn't need a drivers license. The state impounded and sold his truck at a sheriff's auction almost three years ago. It was all done illegally, according to Kurt.

Monday, October 17, 1994.

George DeLuca has not had a very good week. For that matter, the whole year has been lousy. The former New York City cop was busted in March. The feds claimed that George and his wife, Elisa, had been living large in Chesterfield — big house, big pool, big-screen TV, big everything — on the profits of a New York-to-St. Louis drug ring.

The feds had a good case, so George pleaded, "Not Guilty, Just Stupid." He said he didn't speak Spanish, so he had no idea what the Colombians who kept visiting his home were talking about. He said he thought the cash that kept pouring into his house had something to do with his wife's inheritance from the Dominican Republic.

His trial started a few weeks ago. George was free on bond during his trial.

Until this week, that is. Saturday, he withdrew almost $10,000 from the bank, and Monday, during the lunch break, he tried to send, via overnight delivery, most of that money to a girlfriend in New York. Unfortunately for George, the feds had been keeping an eye on him, and they decided he might be getting ready to scram. So his bond was pulled, and George was told that he would be spending his nights in jail.

If Monday was bad, Wednesday was no better.

It was time for closing arguments. Assistant U.S. Attorney Steve Holtshouser went first, and he outlined the case against George and Elisa and a fellow from Colombia who allegedly had supplied the ring with heroin.

It's always difficult, to sit there while the prosecutor sums up the case against you, and it has to be especially difficult if the prosecutor is convincing, and Holtshouser was that.

But after the prosecutor finishes, the defendant normally gets a little boost when his attorney tries to convince the jury that the case isn't really so strong.

Brad Kessler gave George's closing argument. Kessler is a terrific lawyer. In the new parlance of the trade, he's a dream-teamer.

The judge is going to give you an instruction about "deliberate ignorance," Kessler told jurors. That means if you find George was deliberately ignorant about the drug ring, he's still guilty of conspiracy, he said.

Then Kessler, who spoke without notes, got down to business: "You saw George on the witness stand. You heard him. Was there anything deliberate about his ignorance? I don't think so. I think you saw genuine ignorance, true ignorance."

He went on in that vein for a while, and I thought he did remarkably well. Not well enough to get an acquittal maybe, but certainly well enough to make the jurors think, "If I ever get in trouble, I want that guy."

Despite Kessler's eloquence, or maybe because of it, I thought the argument was rough on George. The stupidity defense was his only chance, but still, for a few minutes there, it seemed more like a roast than a trial.

Not that George was the only one who had a rough day in the courtroom Wednesday.

Sam Poston is the young attorney who had been appointed to defend Elisa. Poston didn't even have the stupidity defense to fall back on. Unlike George, Elisa speaks Spanish.

Given the overwhelming evidence against her — even her own daughter had testified against her — what would Poston say?

I figured he might go with the Magna Carta defense. "In 1215 at Runnymede, a group of courageous English nobles agreed to limit the power of the king. Our legal system runs in a straight line from the document they drafted that day to this very courtroom, and it is up to you to continue the tradition of standing up to the power of government ...."

The Magna Carta defense never works, but at least it gives a lawyer something to talk about when he knows he better not mention anything about the evidence.

But Poston decided not to do the Magna Carta. Instead, he looked at the jurors for a long moment - what will he say? I wondered — and he said, "I am a man of few words."

So he kept it short. He mainly argued that Elisa was not guilty of the charge of using a weapon to further the drug conspiracy, and while he did a good job of attacking that issue, that particular charge carries only five years while the drug conspiracy itself carries life.

Chris Hogan, who was defending the Colombian, opted for literature. She read an excerpt from *Alice in Wonderland*.

When Holtshouser returned to conclude his argument, he mainly went after George.

"Nobody's calling George DeLuca a rocket scientist, ladies and gentlemen, but nobody's that dumb," the prosecutor said.

Maybe it was my imagination, but George seemed to sit a little taller after that praise.

If Monday was bad, and Wednesday was bad, Thursday was the worst. George was convicted on all counts. The Colombian was convicted, too, and Elisa was convicted of everything except the gun charge.

Friday, December 8, 1995.

Can Familiarity Breed Skepticism?

The legal problems of James Mattz have never been of great public interest. Mattz, who is 40-years-old, has five felony convictions on his record, and, at the moment, is on probation for a drug conviction.

He went to court 10 days ago on another drug charge. He was charged with possessing a single capsule of heroin.

His trial was not a high-profile trial. It began on a Thursday morning and the testimony was finished by noon. The jury completed its deliberations and rendered its verdict before the afternoon was over.

On one hand, the verdict was not surprising. On the other hand, it was bizarre.

The case began several months ago when Freeman Bosley Sr., alderman of the 3rd Ward and the father of the mayor, was driving the ward's committee woman home. She wanted to change clothes before going to some political event.

There were two men in a car near her home.

"What's up?" one of the men asked Bosley.

"Nothing," said Bosley.

It so happens that these men were parked on a corner that is well-known to the alderman.

"It's the worst corner in the ward," said Bosley. "Not a night goes by that I don't get a call complaining about that corner. Drugs and guns. We've got the Crips right there at the alley, and the Bloods live right around the corner."

Because the corner is known for its drug activity, Bosley figured that if a couple of fellows were sitting in a car hailing strangers, there was a good chance they were trying to buy or sell drugs.

"If somebody says, 'What's up?' as I'm walking out of City Hall, I'd just say, 'Nothing. What's up with you?' I wouldn't think anything of it. But at night on this corner, I'm suspicious," Bosley said.

When the comitteewoman came out of her house, Bosley asked her if she knew the two men in the car. She did not.

So Bosley decided to call the cops and have an officer check out the two men.

Before he could get to a phone, the cops found Bosley. Two officers pulled him over.

"My car was in the shop, and I was driving a loaner. It was a late-model car with Illinois plates. They probably thought I was a gang-banger," Bosley said approvingly.

He recognized one of the cops and quickly told him about the two men in the car. The cops went to the corner.

According to the cops, Mattz appeared to put something in his mouth as the cops approached. The cops ordered the fellows out of the car. As Mattz climbed out, a capsule of heroin fell from his clothes. At least, that's the way the cops told the story.

And that was the state's case against Mattz.

The defense was pretty much limited. If Mattz were to testify, the prosecutor could ask him about his previous convictions, and he'd have to admit that he was on probation for drug possession.

So all the defense could do was put the second guy in the car on the stand. He had only one conviction on his record, and it was a gun charge from a long time ago.

Nevertheless, this second guy wasn't going to be a

great witness. After all, he couldn't swear that Mattz had not put something in his mouth — "As the police approached, were you watching them, or were you watching your friend?"— and he couldn't swear that Mattz had not had a capsule of heroin in his clothes. It would sound pretty silly if he claimed to have frisked him before they went out that night.

Pretty much, then, it was going to be a case in which the jurors either believed the cops, or didn't believe the cops. Maybe they'd think the cops had planted the heroin capsule on Mattz.

There is nothing unusual about a jury facing this kind of decision, but this particular jury was an odd one. One of the jurors was Janet Harmon, wife of Police Chief Clarence Harmon.

How had she gotten on the jury?

In *voir dire*, prosecutor Rachel Smith and public defender Delores Berman questioned her closely. Could she be impartial? Yes, she said. If she were to reach the conclusion that the police officers had not been truthful, would she be willing to acquit? Could she face her husband in that event? Yes and yes, she said.

So she made the jury.

Smith presented the state's case. The alderman and the two cops testified. Berman presented the defense, such as it was. Mainly, she hammered away at inconsistencies between the police report and the officers' testimony.

The jury acquitted Mattz. An acquittal, like a conviction, requires a unanimous vote. In other words, the chief's wife did not believe the cops.

"Doesn't surprise me," said the alderman. "I don't think the chief believes his officers."

The chief and his wife did not return any of my phone calls.

That's too bad. I don't share the alderman's anger, but like the alderman, I'm not really surprised about the chief's wife.

You think my wife trusts reporters?

Sunday, December 11, 1994.

Best Way to Earn Respect?
How about Game of Gin Rummy

Matthew "Mikey" Trupiano, in ill health but free at last, walked into Giuseppe's Restaurant on South Grand one day last week, and a man came up and embraced him. It is, I suppose, an Italian thing, but it reminded me of something you'd see in an old-time, low-budget gangster film.

Which is appropriate. Trupiano has always been a parody of a mobster.

According to the feds, he inherited the leadership of the St. Louis mob after the Leisures and Michaelses blew each other up in the early '80s. They had gone to war after Anthony Giordano, who was a real mobster, died.

It is true that Trupiano was Giordano's nephew. It is true that Trupiano got a big job in Laborers' Local 110. It is true that over the years, the names of the union bosses for 110 and the names of the local chiefs of organized crime have been, for the most part, interchangeable.

But another truth is this: By the time Trupiano allegedly inherited the leadership of our mob, there wasn't much mob to inherit.

Nevertheless, the feds had their collective eye on Trupiano. He was soon busted for running a bookmaking operation.

The trial was a hoot. Nobody came forward to say that Trupiano had broken anybody's legs when they couldn't pay their gambling debts. In fact, it turned out that the biggest money-loser was Trupiano.

That's because he was a gambler himself. Always had been. Before the bookmaking charge, his only run-in with the law had come years ago in Detroit when he was busted at a dice game. He picked up a misdemeanor.

But even if you run a completely honest bookie operation — even a losing one — you're still breaking the law. The feds convicted Trupiano, and he was sent to prison.

He did a year and a half, and came home to his old union job.

The feds, who had clearly been watching too many old gangster movies themselves, were once again determined to get him. They made a deal with a career criminal. In return for getting a pass on some very heavy drug charges, the career criminal would help bring down Trupiano.

Unfortunately for the Elliot Nesses at the federal building, Trupiano was doing nothing illegal. He was being a good family man. He went to work, he went home. In between, he played a lot of gin rummy.

That was enough. The feds busted the game, and charged Trupiano with embezzling from the union — he was playing cards when he should have been working — and participating in an illegal gambling enterprise.

Everyone else in the game got a pass. In fact, it's interesting to note that the game never really stopped, and goes on in a different location, with many of the same players, even today.

Trupiano was convicted, and sentenced to 30 months in federal prison.

His health, never good, deteriorated in prison. His diabetes worsened, he contracted a brain tumor and he had a mild heart attack. So he ended up getting a tour of the federal penal system. He spent stretches in two maximum-security medical facilities, and spent time at two minimum-security camps.

Not surprisingly, he met some interesting characters. He met Lyndon LaRouche, who was doing time for fraud, but is most famous for his conspiracy theories, including the one about the Queen of England heading up an international drug cartel.

"He was a pacer," Trupiano said. "Back and forth, back and forth."

He also met evangelist Jim Bakker, who, like LaRouche, was doing time for fraud. What was Bakker like?

"Hey, I don't associate with guys like that," Trupiano told me. "He stole from old ladies."

He also met a lot of fellow Italians, hard men doing time on serious racketeering charges.

"So you're Trupiano from St. Louis," they'd say. "What are you in for?"

Trupiano resisted the urge to invent something prestigious.

"Gin rummy," he'd say.

The hard men would take a step back.

"Hey, it's your business, Trupiano from St. Louis. If you don't want to talk about it, fine."

"No, really, gin rummy. I was caught playing during working hours," he'd say.

Fortunately, he had the newspaper stories to prove it. The hard men would read the stories with disbelief. So would the guards.

Then, surely, although Trupiano is too modest to say so, the hard men and the guards and all the not-so-hard men would look upon Trupiano with respect. Maybe even fear. If the federal government was so anxious to get Trupiano that it would send him to prison for playing gin rummy, he must be very heavy indeed.

Sunday, October 8, 1995.

S ome defendants clean up well, and what the jury sees is not a low-life criminal but a guy who looks as if he's on his way to an Episcopal church for morning mass.

There was no such problem with Richard L. Sanders when he went to trial last week for the murder of Elizabeth Baker. He wore a tan leisure suit, and his hair was about three inches too long and about 10 years too late to be fashionable, and the whole look was accentuated by a jailhouse tan, which is, of course, no tan at all.

He looked like a burglar.

By the time he was 26, Sanders owned an arrest record that stretched into double figures, and the great majority of those arrests were, in fact, for burglary. Then, eight days after his 27th birthday, he shot Elizabeth Baker to death during an attempt to burglarize a jewelry store at 2646 Cherokee Street.

What an awful plan it was. Sanders and an associate would break into the back of the jewelry store while another man waited in the getaway car about half a block away. This third guy, whose name is Antonio Veal, was supposed to act as a lookout and lay on the horn if a squad car cruised by.

But Veal was so far away that his warning would have been useless. In fact, he was so far away he didn't hear the single gunshot that killed Elizabeth Baker.

She was part owner of the jewelry store. It had been her father's; when he died in November of 1985, half of the store went to his wife and the other half was equally divided among Baker and her seven siblings.

But the store's liabilities were greater than its assets, and when Baker and two brothers agreed to take the store over and take on its debts, they were allowed to do so.

The three new owners were hard workers, and they were in the process of turning things around when Baker was murdered.

Here's how it happened: The jewelry store was very small. Baker heard a noise in the back room and went to see what it was. Sanders shot her in the chest.

Her 3-year-old son was just a few feet away at the time. In addition to her son, she had two little girls, 8 and 6.

In the eyes of the Supreme Court, and in the eyes of holy people like Mother Theresa, every human life has the same value.

But in the eyes of those of us who are less holy, that's not the case. A young mother's life, especially a young mother who was a working person and was working to provide for the children she loved, well, her life is worth more than a lot of other lives.

The homicide cops who worked the Baker shooting certainly felt the same way. I talked to a couple of them before Sanders went on trial. The cops felt more personally involved than they usually do. We're rooting strong for the prosecution, they said.

I sat in on part of the trial, and I could see that it was going well as far as I and the homicide cops were concerned. Ed Rogers, who has handled some very big and very difficult cases, was handling this one for the circuit attorney's office.

Sanders did not have much of a defense. In fact, his attorney used the old two-pronged argument. In the first place, Sanders didn't do it. And second, if he did do it, it was an accident.

Well, the first part of the argument wasn't too strong because both Sanders' partners had told the cops that Sanders did it. In addition, Sanders himself confessed. The videotape of that confession was played to the jury.

The second part of the defense wasn't too strong, either. That's because the gun that was used was a single-action revolver. To fire the gun, the shooter has to pull the hammer back manually before he can pull the trigger. So it would be difficult, to say the least, to unintentionally fire the weapon.

After hearing some of the testimony, I decided to visit the scene of the shooting. The jewelry store had been shut down after Elizabeth Baker's murder, and I wondered what was in the spot now.

It turned out to be a watch repair shop.

I went in and explained to the young man at the counter, whose name is Richard Allen, that I was a reporter. He took me into the back room and showed me the spot where Baker had been shot.

I told Allen that I had a Timex watch that was broken. It's probably not worth getting repaired, I said. Bring it in and let us take a look at it, he said. So I drove home and got my watch.

The next day, which was Thursday, the jury convicted Richard L. Sanders of first-degree murder. But I wasn't in the courtroom when the jury came back with its verdict. I was at the watch repair shop picking up my watch.

Allen's wife, Cheryl, who is a young working woman and perhaps not unlike Elizabeth Baker, handed me the watch. The charge was $8.

They did a very nice job.

Monday, July 20, 1987.

For Two Detectives, a
Labor of Love: Avenging Elissa

Mike Flaherty is a real estate agent these days, and Bill Roach is a sergeant in the Second District, which is the quietest district in the city.

They used to be partners in the Juvenile Division. They specialized in low-profile cases. They did a lot of runaways.

When 11-year-old Elissa Self-Braun disappeared on her way to a school bus in January of 1991, Flaherty and Roach were told to find her.

Five days after her disappearance, her body was found under a bridge in the St. Francis River in Wayne County. Her body had been removed from the river and taken to a funeral home by the time the detectives arrived. She was lying on a table, still caked with mud. Roach went up to the table and ran his hand through the young girl's hair.

"We never stopped looking for you, honey," he said, "and we'll never stop looking for the guy who did this."

Normally, the case would have been turned over to the homicide section, but because the body had been found in Wayne County, the case did not officially belong to the city.

But the two detectives, working mostly on their own time, were allowed to conduct the investigation.

It was a labor of love. Flaherty and Roach both had daughters only slightly older than Elissa.

The two detectives were determined to find the murderer, but they didn't get carried away with their determination. Shortly after Elissa's body was discovered, a woman from Wayne County called. The night before the body was found, her former son-in-law had come to Wayne County to visit his children, the woman said. He had just gotten out of prison.

What was he in prison for? the detectives asked.

He raped a 6-year-old, the woman said.

It turned out he lived in an apartment less than a mile from Elissa's house. The detectives interrogated him for 10 hours and then let him go.

"We wanted it to be him, but we realized he wasn't the guy," Roach said.

They sent details of the crime to the FBI, which sent back a psychological profile of the man they should be looking for.

They talked to their colleagues in the sex-crimes division, and they checked out dozens of names. They worked on their vacations. They worked at night.

One of the potential suspects fit the profile almost exactly. A loner and a convicted sex offender, he was already in jail, charged with committing a couple of robberies and three sexual attacks in a two-week period. Elissa had disappeared during that two weeks.

Flaherty went to talk to the guy's father, who lived in an apartment on the city's South Side. Through the screen door, Flaherty commented that the man's accent gave him away. You weren't raised in the city, Flaherty said.

Nope. Raised in Ellsinore, the man said.

Flaherty's throat went dry. That town is very near where Elissa's body was found.

Hey, I'm a canoeist, Flaherty said. I used to float the St. Francis River down there.

The man invited Flaherty in. They talked about float trips. The man said his son used to float the St. Francis. Where did he put in? Flaherty asked. The man described a little park under a bridge. It was, Flaherty realized, where the killer had dumped Elissa's body.

Flaherty and Roach then searched their suspect's car, which the police were already holding. They found tiny flecks of blood in a vaseline jar. They already had semen specimens that had been collected during the examination of the girl's body.

But the police department balked at paying for expensive DNA testing. After all, this wasn't officially a city case.

"We'll have a bake sale," the detectives threatened, and the higher-ups backed down. The department paid for the DNA tests, and the tests indicated that the flecks of blood matched Elissa, and the semen matched the suspect.

Last week, the suspect, Martin Link, was convicted of murder, and Saturday, a jury sentenced him to death.

A couple of nights later, Roach, Flaherty and prosecutor Joe Warzycki got together for a couple of beers. Warzycki, who also has a teenage daughter, had taken the case personally, too, but he's already gearing up for his next murder trial. For Roach and Flaherty, though, this was it. The case that had consumed their lives for more than four years was over.

"It was an honor to work this case," Flaherty said.

Oddly enough, the two detectives never got much credit. On the day Elissa's body was found, the Gulf War began. On the day that Link was charged with murder, the hard-line Communists in Russia staged a coup.

But the detectives have gotten more recognition than they ever expected. After the jurors imposed the death sentence, they asked to see the two detectives.

Roach and Flaherty walked into the room, and the jurors applauded.

"I looked around to see who was behind us," Roach said. "Then I realized it was for us."

Friday, August 18, 1995.

Of Bobby Lee Griffin, "Honor" and "Home"

Through the Plexiglas window, I saw Bobby Lee Griffin come shuffling down the hall, and the first thing I thought was this: I've seen dead guys who looked healthier.

The second thing I thought was this: The leg irons are unnecessary.

He was leaning on a walker for support. An IV bottle hung above the walker and a tube ran from the bottle to his arm. His face was a mass of bruises and welts. The cops had worked him over good.

I picked up the phone and watched him pick up the matching phone on the prisoners' side of the window.

"You look good," I said.

Maybe he smiled. It was impossible to tell.

"It was a setup," he said.

This is a strange world, and anything is possible, but setup or not, Griffin was walking down an alley behind his sworn enemy's house at 2 in the morning with a .44 Magnum revolver in his waistband. The revolver was loaded. And hot. It came from a burglary in St. Genevieve.

"I had the gun in my waistband, and when the cops jumped out, my first thought was to throw the gun away. They must have seen me pull the gun and gotten the wrong idea. I don't suppose you can blame them," he said.

He's lucky to be alive, I thought.

Regular readers might remember Bobby Lee Griffin. He got out of prison this summer after serving almost 34 years. He originally went in on a murder charge, and then, while he was in, he killed an inmate. The inmate was his brother-in-law, and Griffin killed him because he had been an abusive husband to Griffin's sister.

So Griffin missed all of the '60s, all of the '70s and all of the '80s. This was going to be his first Christmas on the outside since the Christmas of 1957.

"Was" is the operative word in that last sentence.

In addition to the absolute certainty of having his parole revoked, Griffin faces a host of new charges. There's the federal charge of being a felon in possession of a firearm and the state charge of carrying a concealed weapon. The fact that the weapon was stolen translates into receiving stolen property. There's probably more — resisting arrest comes to mind — but all that is legal stuff and can best be left to the lawyers.

As I looked at Griffin, I thought about three conversations I've had recently. Not with Griffin, but about him.

The first conversation was with a guy who served time with Griffin. I asked about the murder of the brother-in-law.

"All of Bobby Lee's friends knew that the guy had beaten up Bobby Lee's sister. So when the guy got to prison, Bobby Lee had to do something," the man explained.

Of course. Honor and all that. This code of conduct certainly explains what Griffin was doing in the alley with a revolver Wednesday morning. He had been feuding with his 35-year-old daughter's boyfriend. She's a former prostitute and drug addict — at least she says that stuff is in her past — and all of Griffin's friends knew that the boyfriend had beaten up Griffin's daughter.

The second conversation was with a guy who had been with Griffin a couple of days before the arrest.

"I had the radio on to some Christmas music. Bobby Lee asked me to change stations. He said the music made him sad. It reminded him of his childhood, and I don't know if you know it, but he had a very rough childhood," the man said.

The third conversation was with one of the cops involved in the arrest.

"We got a call at about 2 in the morning that Bobby Lee had been up in the apartment with a gun. By the time we got over there, he was gone. But we had two squad cars in plain view in the parking lot behind the building when Bobby Lee came up the alley. It wasn't like we were hiding, or he was sneaking," the cop said.

He went down swinging. Again, he lived up to his code.

Incidentally, the cop attributed the severity of Griffin's injuries to a fall.

"A lot of gravel and stuff in the alley. I guess he fell right on his face," the cop said.

When Griffin and I finished our conversation, I told him to put me on his visitors' list when he gets transferred from the hospital to the jail, where he will await his parole revocation or his new trials, whichever comes first.

After I hung up the phone, I lingered at the window and watched a guard lead Griffin down the hall. The leg irons were unnecessary, but they added a nice touch. Hobbled like an animal, I thought.

Still, there was no reason to feel sad. Bobby Lee Griffin was in custody. In a true sense, he had come home for Christmas.

Sunday, December 20, 1992.

Ethnic Assault Ends Dreams of Refugee Who Fled Vietnam

S ometime in the late 1930s, a Chinese farmer, fleeing the Japanese Army, took his family and crossed the border into Vietnam. He settled in the village of Hai Ninh, near the port city of Haiphong.

The family was very poor, but the father decided that one of his children would be educated. He chose his youngest son. The boy learned to read and write. He was eventually able to leave the fields and go to work for the French.

By the time Dien Bien Phu fell in 1954, signaling the end of French occupation in the northern half of the country, the boy was a young man with a family of his own. Fearing retaliation from the communist victors, the young man and his family fled south. They settled in the village of Song Mao near the city of Phan Thiet.

When the Americans came, the young man went to work for them. So did many of his 11 children, 10 of whom were boys.

One of these boys was Ha A Chi.

When the North Vietnamese Army rolled into Saigon in 1975, Chi feared that this connections with the American Army would make him a marked man. For more than a year, he lay low.

In June of 1977, he managed to escape Vietnam on a fishing boat. With no captain and no compass, he and his comrades sailed toward Singapore. After nine days, they reached their destination, but were not allowed to land. They sailed to Malaysia.

Because he had served with the Americans, he was allowed to emigrate to this country. He arrived in 1978. Originally, he was sent to Virginia, but he came to St. Louis later that year. He worked at a chop suey house on West Florissant.

The next year, he married an American girl. For the next 17 years, he lived a hard-scrabble version of the American dream. He and his wife bought a small house in Bridgeton. They had a daughter — she's now 17 - and they sent her to a private Christian school. Chi worked as a cook. Long hours in hot kitchens. He was known, former colleagues say, for singing and whistling as he worked in front of the stove. And he worked six days a week.

Until a Sunday evening in May of 1996.

Chi had just finished a 10-hour shift at a Chinese restaurant in Manchester. He was sitting on a curb outside a convenience store waiting for his wife to pick him up.

A 27-year-old man named Thomas Hampton spotted him. According to the police report, Hampton was drunk.

"I'll kill you, you blanking Chink," Hampton shouted, and then he charged.

At 6 foot 1 and 180 pounds, Hampton towered over Chi. By the time witnesses restrained Hampton, Chi was on the ground, bleeding from his ears and head.

"I kicked that blanking gook's ass," Hampton told the cops.

Chi has not worked since the attack. He has had four surgeries to repair the damage, and more surgeries are planned, but the most severe damage — a brain injury — seems to be beyond the reach of modern medicine. He has been declared disabled by the Social Security Administration.

"From a pure cognitive point of view and an intellectual/personality point of view, he is not the same person he was before this," one doctor wrote.

While waiting for Chi's disability payments to begin, the family went on AFDC. Twice, the Bridgeton Community Helping Ministry has had to step in to stop foreclosure on the family's house.

"Our dreams are gone," Chi's wife, Mimi, told me Monday night. "He always wanted to open his own restaurant."

Tuesday morning, Hampton appeared before Circuit Judge Philip Sweeney. Pursuant to a plea bargain, he had agreed to plead guilty to second-degree assault and ethnic intimidation. He would get a four-year sentence on each count, the sentences to run concurrently. Hampton will probably have to serve about a third of his four-year sentence.

He was dressed in khaki pants and a blue blazer. He was flanked by two private attorneys. His parents and an older brother sat quietly in the back row of the courtroom.

How strange it is, I thought, the way things turn out. Hampton is a rich kid from Ladue, a graduate of Country Day.

The judge asked him — a routine question — about the extent of his education, and he told the judge that he has two bachelor degrees from St. Louis University. He stood quietly as Chi read a victim's impact statement.

"I came here to be free," Chi said in a halting voice. "I know I have to work very hard. My dream is to open a restaurant and send my daughter to college. For 18 years, I work very hard to make this happen.

"I'm glad I'm an American," he said in conclusion.

Hampton then asked for permission to address Chi.

"I feel so bad I can't express it," he said. "I am truly sorry."

As the deputies took the child of privilege out the back door, the child of refugees went out the front. There were shattered dreams in both directions, as far as the eye could see.

Wednesday, June 11, 1997.

Movie Script Plays Poorly in Real Life

Jason Barr was a young man who thought life was a movie, and in this movie, he was a desperado on the run from the law.

So he came to St. Louis from his hometown of Sedalia, Mo. He carried a pistol in a shoulder holster, just the way a desperado is supposed to. He drank shots of tequila, just the way a desperado is supposed to. Truth is, though, Barr wasn't a tough guy. He was a middle-class kid living a fantasy life. He was writing the script as he went along.

Only if you were willing to stretch things a bit could you say he was on the run from the law. His driver's license had been revoked because of a DWI, and later he was stopped and charged with driving on a revoked license.

So sure, he was a desperado if you consider a traffic charge to be a big deal.

He ran all the way to St. Louis, and his cousin agreed to put him up. She was sharing an apartment with a young man, and there were several other young people who drifted in and out of the place.

These were mostly young people who were in the process of, as the saying goes, finding themselves. Like Barr, they were middle class kids.

One night, for no apparent reason other than the fact that he couldn't handle the shots of tequila he was drinking, Barr pulled his pistol out of his shoulder holster and walked over to his cousin's boyfriend, who was asleep on the couch.

Barr shot the young man in the head.

It was a senseless murder.

Barr wrote a goofy note to his cousin, urging her to "hide the body." Then he took his victim's car, and drove back to Sedalia.

He was promptly arrested.

His family hired a lawyer, and the lawyer advised him not to make any statements. But Barr broke down on the way from Sedalia to St. Louis.

Teary-eyed and emotionally distraught, the desperado confessed.

The case went to trial last week.

Barr's victim was the son of a friend of mine, so for my friend's sake, I was hoping that Barr would seem as evil as the thing he had done.

Even Barr's attorney, the illustrious Charlie Shaw, was thinking along the same lines.

"I know what your friend is going through," Shaw said. "I lost a kid, too. Mine died in an accident. Maybe it would have been easier if I would have had somebody to hate."

Maybe hating would make it easier, but in this instance, that's not the way it worked out.

Barr, who is now 21, was more pitiful than sinister. He claimed the police were lying about his confession, and he claimed that his gun had gone off accidentally during a struggle.

As he testified about this struggle, it was as if he were still writing a script. He was more or less winging it as he went along.

He wasn't a credible witness.

Even Shaw won't be able to salvage this one, I thought.

On the morning when closing arguments were to be heard, the deputies led Barr into the courtroom. As he was led to his seat, he flashed a smile to his mom.

In that moment, I could see the kid as he must have

been years ago, back when he was his mother's darling, back when life wasn't a movie about desperados on the run.

His mom, who seemed like a very nice lady, smiled back.

Shaw was, as usual, very eloquent. He said the concept of self-defense honored our Constitution. He said some other fine things, too, but frankly, his client had already convicted himself.

The only real defense would have been the truth. The late teens and early twenties are a dangerous time for young men. Sometimes they think life is a movie.

But the law doesn't allow for an argument like that. As far as the law is concerned, a crime is a crime.

Shirley Loepker, the prosecutor, explained to the jury that this particular crime was first-degree murder. She talked about victims, and their families.

As Loepker finished her closing argument, Barr's mother began crying softly. Maybe she was crying because of what her son had done, or maybe she was crying because she could guess the outcome of the trial, or maybe it was a combination of both.

Maybe only a mother could understand her grief.

When the jury left the courtroom, Barr's mother began sobbing.

My friend's wife — her name is Carol Rose — stood up and walked over to Barr's mother. Carol put her arms around Barr's mother, and the two women embraced.

Barr's mother was almost hysterical. Carol kept hugging her, trying to comfort her.

Through such kindness, she honors the memory of her slain son, I thought.

The jury came back in two hours. They found Barr guilty of first-degree murder. That will mean life without parole.

In a way, it didn't matter. The verdict seemed anti-climactic.

Barr had been wrong. The movie isn't about desperados, and tequila, and shoulder holsters. Shaw and I had been wrong, too. The movie isn't about hate.

Only Carol was right. If life is a movie, it's supposed to be about love.

Sunday, July 1, 1990.

Picking through the Pieces of Driftwood

When Scott Shockley, who had just turned 17, was shot in the head while working the drive-through window at a fast-food restaurant on Hampton Avenue, the cops had absolutely nothing to go on.

Because Shockley was not expected to live, the case was turned over to the homicide unit. Early on the morning after the shooting, two homicide detectives, Mike Lauer and Ralph Campbell, visited the hospital. Shockley had just spent eight hours in surgery. The prognosis was not good.

After talking to the family, the detectives concluded that the one avenue that offered the most potential was shut down.

"We pretty much felt that the kid didn't have any enemies, at least the kind who would do something like this," Campbell said.

Had there been a feud over a girlfriend or a fight at school, the cops would have had some place to start.

If life were a movie, there would have been something like that. In the movies, detectives are always matching wits with clever criminals.

But in real life, it usually isn't like that. Most street criminals aren't clever. Instead, the tides of their lives continually wash them onto the shores of justice and then the system throws them back into the sea like pieces of driftwood and then, not too much later, they wash ashore again.

The trick is to pick through the driftwood and figure out who did what.

On the morning after the shooting, about an hour after Lauer and Campbell left the hospital, a 32-year-old man named Ozie Collins washed ashore in Hazelwood.

The Combined Urban Fugitive Force, a cooperative effort between the U.S. marshals and local municipalities, went to a house looking for a woman wanted on drug charges. While they were talking to their suspect, they heard a noise in another room. They found Collins. He had a gun in his waistband.

When a computer check revealed that he had a prior felony conviction, he was arrested on the federal charge of felon in possession of a weapon.

At the federal holdover, another U.S. marshal noticed that Collins looked very much like a man in a photo that the FBI had been distributing. The photo had been taken by a surveillance camera during a bank robbery.

The FBI, by the way, makes sure that its photographs get wide distribution at jails and holdovers and police stations. The agency is well aware that criminals are constantly washing ashore.

This particular photo had been remarkably clear. In fact, several people had called to say that the guy in the photo was the man who had robbed them. One of these victims had been robbed in a fast-food restaurant on Hampton.

Late that same evening, two 4th District detectives, Dave Doetzel and Brian McGlynn, were driving in the area of O'Fallon Place. The neighborhood has been the scene of a series of rapes and robberies.

Shortly after midnight, the detectives noticed a car with expired plates. The detectives stopped the car. Two men and a woman were inside.

As the detectives approached, they noticed the driver pass something to the man in the back seat. When the detectives checked the back seat, they saw a gun.

They ordered everybody out of the car. When the guy in the back seat got out, he went behind the woman and suddenly grabbed her around the neck, using her as a shield. Then he threw her to the ground and took off running.

The detectives ran after him. The other man and the woman jumped back in the car and sped away, but their escape didn't really matter. The detectives already had the drivers license and, anyway, he would probably wash ashore within a few days.

Eventually, the detectives caught the guy they were chasing. "I don't want to eat the gun charge," he said. "I can give you something big."

What he had to give was two names — Ozie and C.K. These are the guys who did the shooting at the chicken store, he said. They were also involved in a jewelry store robbery, he said.

The district detectives notified the homicide detectives.

By this time, the homicide guys knew that the feds had a man named Ozie who was a suspect in a fast-food robbery near the chicken store. That part of the puzzle was beginning to come together. But C.K. was still a mystery. Actually, C.K. is not an uncommon nickname. It generally stands for Crip Killer.

On Saturday night, five days after the shooting, the district detectives talked to an informer. He knew of a Baby C.K. The guy's name was either Curtis McKnight or Pat McKnight.

Everybody started looking for him.

Wednesday afternoon, Shockley had recovered enough to look at a photo of a lineup that had been held for the victims of the earlier robberies. Collins was in the lineup. The homicide detectives showed him the photograph, and he cringed.

"Don't let him hurt me," he said. Then he regained his composure and pointed to Collins.

"That's the man who shot me," he said.

He also picked out Curtis McKnight's photograph from a photo spread. He identified McKnight as the man who had been with Collins.

That same day, the district detectives called McKnight's grandmother. McKnight answered the phone. The detectives asked him to come to the station. He said he couldn't. "Come on over," he said. "I'm on the third floor."

It sounded like a setup, but this is what these guys do for a living. They went to the apartment on North Kingshighway and climbed the stairs.

McKnight was waiting for them. They arrested him without incident.

He denied taking part in any jewelry store robberies or bank robberies, and the district detectives didn't talk to him about the shooting. He did, however, explain his nickname. He had been Baby C.K. until the real C.K. was shot and killed earlier this year. At that point, McKnight dropped the Baby prefix.

The last time McKnight had washed ashore was in the summer of 1990, when a SCAT team arrested him for selling crack. He was given probation.

When the district detectives were finished with him, he was turned over to homicide. "Curtis made statements naming himself and implicating another," said a homicide sergeant, who would not discuss the details of McKnight's statement.

Thursday, warrants were issued charging Collins and

McKnight with attempted first-degree robbery and armed criminal action.

As a footnote, the man who had first given police the names of Ozie and C.K. was released after spending 20 hours in the holdover. Three days later, he was tentatively identified as a man who exchanged shots with a cop near Carr Square.

He has not yet washed ashore.

November 17, 1991.

Violent History Plays Out Today

Fifty years ago, long before the word "dysfunctional" came into vogue, there was a family in St. Ann of whom the operative word, old-fashioned as it may sound now, was "strange."

The mother was extremely quiet, and the father was an immigrant who spoke almost no English. He worked as a redcap at Union Station.

The three little girls were also very, very quiet.

Rosie was the middle child. She got married before she finished high school — which wasn't so strange in those days — but the marriage didn't work, and when Rosie was pregnant with her second child, she and her husband separated.

Years later, the children would recall Rosie as an absentee mother. She was there, but she wasn't. Rosie remarried, and had another child, but she was still somehow absent.

The oldest child, a girl who was 5 years old when the third baby was born, functioned as the woman of the house. She was in charge of taking care of the baby, and when she would come home from school, she would fix dinner. Most often, she simply opened a couple of cans of food. Meanwhile, Rosie would lock herself in her bedroom and read romance novels.

Rosie's new husband was violent. One day he threw a kitten against the wall and killed it.

Rosie divorced him, and married again. As far as the children were concerned, the new husband was even worse. His anger, they say, was most often directed at the youngest boy. Eventually, he and Rosie were divorced.

The middle child, a little boy, was rescued. A childhood friend of Rosie's took him in. This woman's name is R'Neill Wells. The little boy she took in is now a young man, and he's doing fine.

The oldest girl was not rescued. She stayed with Rosie, and she grew up to be a troubled woman. At last count, she had been married five times.

The youngest boy was not rescued, either. In fact, Rosie sent him back to his father, the violent man who had once killed a kitten. This boy grew up to be a very troubled young man.

His name is Daniel Basile.

None of the adults who shaped him showed up at his recent trial in Cape Girardeau. He was convicted of murdering Elizabeth DeCaro. He was hired to do the job by Richard Decaro, Elizabeth's husband.

Basile had been convicted once before of this murder. The first time was in state court, and the public defender's office brought Rosie in from Florida to testify for her son in the penalty phase of that trial. When it was her turn to testify, she couldn't be found.

"Once again, Danny has been abandoned by his mother," the public defender said.

Basile was sentenced to death.

Later, when he was indicted by the federal government, the feds talked about a deal. If he would agree to testify against DeCaro, the state would agree to change his sentence from death to life. Basile would not take the deal.

"This was the first time in his life that he ever felt important or that he had any control over anything," R'Neill told me. "He can control his own death."

R'Neill, incidentally, did attend the trial in Cape Girardeau.

Her stepson, Craig Wells, was involved in the case, too. He had worked for DeCaro, and when DeCaro had asked him if he knew anyone who would be willing to steal a van as part of an insurance scam, Wells had suggested Basile. That's how DeCaro and Basile got together.

"I feel very badly about Craig's involvement," R'Neill said.

Because he had been raised with Basile's half brother - the middle child whom R'Neill had rescued - Wells considered Basile to be a brother. When Basile had no place to live, Wells took him in. In the weeks before the murder, Basile was sleeping on the couch in the small trailer Wells shared with his girlfriend and her three daughters.

When DeCaro, who was all the things that Basile wasn't and had all the things that Basile didn't, offered him $15,000 to join the partnership in murder, Basile agreed.

Before the verdict Thursday night, Basile undid the rubber band that held his hair in a pony tail - he had refused to cut his hair for the trial - and let it flow down over his shoulders. As he was walked out of the courtroom, he whistled a haunting melody.

Later, he called R'Neill. He said the song was called "The Death March," and he said he whistled it to irritate DeCaro. He did not care that he had been convicted again, he told her, as long as DeCaro had been convicted, too.

DeCaro's story might be more complicated - is more complicated - but Basile was a dead-end kid, and all roads led him to where he is today.

Sadly, though, the story does not end here. While he was staying at Wells' trailer, Basile had a brief fling with a 16-year-old girl who lived in a nearby trailer.

While Basile was in jail awaiting his first trial, the 16-year-old gave birth to his child.

Sunday, March 10, 1996

Unrepentant Man with a Big Heart

I don't regret anything," said Michael Mulikey. "In the end, you answer to The Man upstairs."

He was standing outside Division 26 at the Municipal Courts building Friday morning. An assortment of people wandered past him into the courtroom. Everybody was relaxed. The docket was for people charged with misdemeanor offenses. Nobody goes to prison for a misdemeanor.

So relaxed is the atmosphere at the misdemeanor docket that a good number of defendants don't bother even to show up. That rule held true Friday.

Judy Moss was among those who didn't show up.

"I didn't figure she'd show up," said Mulikey.

Of course not. Moss has a lengthy arrest record, mostly for prostitution. She knows the system. She understands that if you don't show up for the misdemeanor docket, it isn't as if the cops will come looking for you.

The cops will wait until they pick you up for something new. Then the new charges will be piled on top of the old charges.

Mulikey understands, too. He used to be a cop. He retired last November after 22 years on the force.

He first met Moss a couple of years ago.

"She was eight months pregnant, and still working the streets." he said. "You remember something like that."

About a month later, he ran into her again. She was standing on Cherokee Street. Somebody had just beaten the tar out of her.

"I asked her about the baby, and she said the state had taken it away from her. Apparently, the baby had been born addicted to cocaine. She told me she wanted

63

to straighten herself out and get her baby back," Mulikey said.

Mulikey went home, and told his wife the story. They decided to try to help. So they brought the young woman into their home.

"You know cops," he said. "There were a lot of stories. Me and Moss. My wife and Moss. My wife and me and Moss."

The young woman stayed with them only about a week. One day, she just disappeared. So did Mulikey's off-duty gun, and about $80.

Mulikey reported the theft.

About a week later, Moss showed up at the Mulikeys' home, asking for another chance.

"If I get my gun back, I won't prosecute," Mulikey told her.

So Moss told the detectives who were handling the theft case that she had traded the gun for crack cocaine at a drug house. The people at the drug house told the detectives that the fellow who had ended up with the gun had gone to Kansas City, but was expected back in St. Louis in just a few days.

Needless to say, this news did not endear Mulikey to his superiors.

"As soon as the crack-heads are finished with the gun, they promise to return it."

Which is exactly what happened. The fellows at the drug house, happy to cooperate, turned Mulikey's gun over to the detectives.

Meanwhile, the Mulikeys had taken Moss in again, and had enrolled her in a substance-abuse program.

Incidentally, the cops ran ballistic tests on Mulikey's gun to determine if it had been used in any open shootings here or in Kansas City while it was out of Mulikey's possession. It had not been.

Moss dropped out of the substance-abuse program, and went back to crack cocaine. The Mulikeys kicked her out of their home.

Nevertheless, the police department was still unhappy about the whole situation.

Mulikey was suspended for 10 days for associating with a known felon.

That would have been the end of the story except that last week Moss showed up again at the Mulikeys' house. She was in bad shape. Among her complaints was open sores in her mouth. Syphilis, thought Mulikey.

He agreed to take her to Regional hospital.

But no way would he and his wife take her in again. No more chances.

After the doctors checked her at the hospital — it wasn't syphilis — she asked for a ride back to the South Side. OK, said Mulikey.

Her clothes were filthy and torn. Could she possibly "borrow" a blouse?

That would be up to his wife, Mulikey said. When they got back to the Mulikeys' house, Moss asked to use the bathroom. Mulikey went upstairs to talk to his wife.

When he came back downstairs, Moss was gone. So was some money. So was some jewelry. So was his gun.

"She knew where we kept things," Mulikey told me.

She was arrested the next day. The new stealing charges were piled on top of four charges that were already pending against her. She told detectives that she had traded Mulikey's gun for some crack cocaine. The cops filed the case as a felony, but the circuit attorney's office issued it as a misdemeanor.

"The major factor in reducing the charge has to do with credibility," said Steve Ohmer, who heads the warrant office. "The victim and the suspect were acquaintances. That muddies the water."

Mulikey doesn't think it should. He said that Moss needs to go to prison to get off crack cocaine. "I think it would help her. You know, that's all we ever tried to do."

I asked him if he felt at all foolish. He shook his head. "It's like I told you. At the end, you have to answer to The Man upstairs," he said.

Sunday, September 5, 1993

Judgement: A Call of Poor Judgement

The court of public opinion, the honorable Judge William McClellan presiding, is again in session. Today's case is a bit different from most of the cases we hear. That's because this case will be going to an honest-to-goodness court in St. Louis County later this month. "Objection, your honor! When you first began conducting this so-called court, you promised you would not handle cases that were still in the judicial pipeline. The pre-trial publicity isn't fair to the parties involved."

Objection overruled! I'm the judge here! Besides, it's the exception that proves the rule. I read that somewhere. Most important, in this particular case, we will be considering evidence that the real court would surely consider immaterial. And because this case will be going to a real court, I will go out of my way to be fair and impartial. Now back to the case.

Our client - I mean, one of the parties involved - is Ron Peterson. He is suing the city of Des Peres.

Let me tell you a little about Peterson.

He is out there in the Great Hustle, which is, of course, the place a person finds himself when he or she is trying to make ends meet without the benefit of a regular job.

Peterson had two little hustles going in the Great Hustle. He was a shade-tree mechanic, and he did auto repossessions.

His story, as far as we're concerned, begins in mid-January of 1986. In his role as a shade-tree mechanic, he was trying to fix a 1967 Nova, but he needed a new engine. He had an assistant, and this assistant knew a guy who said he knew a guy who had a similar car he wanted to sell.

This friend of the assistant turned out to be David Diaz, who was later to gain a certain notoriety for being the burglar who escaped from city jail with a man awaiting trial for murder. But that's beside the point except to warn you not to be surprised that the car Peterson obtained happened to be hot.

So the police caught Peterson lifting the engine from a stolen car. He was arrested and taken to jail. Meanwhile, Peterson's assistant and Diaz took Peterson's car, a 1973 Plymouth, and drove to Des Peres, where another friend lived.

The police stopped the car on a traffic violation, and the officer discovered, in the back seat, a number of tools that are used for breaking into automobiles. The police then impounded the car.

For almost a year and a half, Peterson has been trying to get his tools back.

Peterson, incidentally, pleaded guilty to fourth-degree tampering, which is a misdemeanor. He received two years of unsupervised probation.

Now the case we are concerned with boils down to this: Should the city of Des Peres give Peterson his tools back?

The city's best argument is that the tools - your standard slim jims, picks, etc. - are used for only one thing, and that is breaking into cars. The city can also point out that Peterson happened to be in jail on a charge relating to a stolen auto at the exact time the cops confiscated the tools.

Peterson's best argument is that in addition to the tools, there were some repossession orders in the car. Those orders were from a couple of used car dealers as well as a bank. A person often needs to break into a car in order to repossess it.

As far as the tampering charge is concerned, Peterson says he is guilty of bad judgment. "I'll never buy another car without a title," he says.

That's basically the case the jury will hear. By the way, Peterson will be representing himself. He can't afford an attorney.

But let's forget attorneys and evidence. In this court, where anything that strikes me as interesting is considered admissible, I'd like to point out somethings I found in Peterson's apartment. I visited him twice, once unannounced, during a week when his wife and four children were visiting her parents. (Her parents paid for the trip.)

First of all, it's not a fancy apartment. There is not even a telephone. But the place was neat.

On one wall in the kitchen was a hand-lettered sign that read, "There can be no happiness if the things we believe in are different from the things we do." Taped to the refrigerator was a free-verse poem about mothers that read in part, "A mother is not here to do things you can do for yourself. A mother is here to do what you cannot do." On another wall in the kitchen was something called "A Parent's Prayer" that asked for divine help in raising children.

In the small hall between the kitchen and the living room, children's papers from school were taped to the wall, as were a couple of slogans exhorting the children to work hard in school.

In the living room, tacked to a wall, was "A letter from Jesus," and a series of slogans about children, called "Children Learn What They Live."

As I started to leave the apartment, I noticed that Peterson's wife had taped a list of things to do while she was gone. Some of them were the standard things - do dishes, take out the garbage - but a couple of others dealt with the family dog, a mixed breed named Cleo. One of the items on the list said, "Give Cleo lots of attention, and put the bread in the refrigerator because Cleo will chew on it to punish you for leaving her alone."

I'm a sucker for slogans and dogs and cheap little apartments where signs of love are everywhere.

Therefore, based on what he saw in the apartment, Judge McClellan rules that Des Peres should return the tools to Peterson, and let him earn some money repossessing cars.

Monday, August 17, 1987

II

Slogging

Getting an Angle on Ann Landers

Ann Landers was easy to spot.

She looked just like her picture. Hair flipped up and all. A smile that seemed familiar because I'd seen it so many times on top of her column. I was going to walk right over to her table, but then I had an inspiration. Ms. Landers' table was within a few feet of the maître d's stand, and I knew that anything I said to the maitre d would be overheard by the people at the table. So what I said is this: "The Howard party, please."

Howard happens to be the last name of Ms. Landers' son-in-law. By asking for the Howard party instead of the Landers party, I'd ingratiate myself with Mr. Howard. I figured it must be difficult having a mother-in-law who makes a living dispensing advice. Maybe I could establish some kind of rapport with the guy and get him to talk about what it's like having Ann Landers as a mother-in-law.

That would make a clever little story, I thought.

I suppose I should back up a little.

My editors had sent me to interview Ms. Landers. They explained she was in St. Louis for her daughter's birthday, and the three of them — Ms. Landers, her daughter, Margo, and her son-in-law, Ken Howard — would be having dinner Wednesday night in the Terrace Room of the Sheraton Plaza Hotel. I was expected at 8 p.m.

Frankly, the assignment had come as a surprise. Editors tend to classify reporters as far as the kinds of stories they think the reporters handle best. I'm assigned to the night cop beat. My editors think I relate best to cops and bondsmen and everyday people like that. This was the first time I'd been assigned a celebrity interview since I joined the newspaper staff a couple of years ago, and I knew the editors didn't expect much.

"Just give us a few inches of copy to go with a photo," they said.

That's what I had planned on doing until the son-in-law angle hit me. Frankly, I hadn't even been sure what questions I was going to ask Ms. Landers. I often read her column, but I also often read the daily horoscope, and I tend to think of the two in similar terms. That is, I think she's fun to read, but I don't take her advice too seriously.

At any rate, when I asked for the Howard party, the maitre d gave me a strange look and told me I was standing next to their table.

I introduced myself and sat down.

"You're Mr. Howard, of course," I said.

He flashed a brilliant smile and nodded. While he grinned, I studied him, the way a leopard studies a deer. He was a big man, and strikingly handsome, but I didn't hold it against him. Everybody can't be blessed, as I am, with average size and average looks.

"You're from St. Louis, I take it?" I asked.

The brilliant smile dulled. He said he was from Connecticut.

"Well, let me get a little background information," I said. "How long have you lived here?"

The smile was completely gone. He said something about being in St. Louis for a tribute.

"A tribute for whom?" I asked, trying to sound more in control than I felt.

He said "Tribute" was a play.

"You must be an actor, then," I said.

"This is unbelievable," he said angrily. He started rattling off credits. He told me he was the star of "White Shadow." His voice rose as he said something about how he had played Thomas Jefferson in some play I had never heard of.

Things were going badly, but I tried to regroup.

" 'White Shadow,' wasn't that a television show or something?" I asked.

He said something to Ms. Landers about how he didn't have to put up with this, and he started to stand up. I began to apologize and tried to explain that I almost never watch television. This interview will just take a couple of minutes, I said. What I'd really like to do is just talk informally for a couple of minutes, I said. Maybe just listen to the conversation.

"I only do that when I'm paid for it, or when the cameras are rolling," he said. He told Ms. Landers he'd return when I left, and off he went.

Deciding to drop the son-in-law angle, I started asking Ms. Landers some inane questions. I mentioned something about recycling columns and asked her if she wrote her own letters.

Ms. Landers said she receives 1,000 letters a day and said it was absurd to think she'd write her own letters. I agreed it was absurd, and said I certainly didn't think she wrote her own letters. I've always considered that an absurd contention, I said.

Her daughter, Margo, started whining.

"Ken's really angry, Mom," she said.

"Maybe I'd better leave," I said, but Ms. Landers was extremely gracious and told me to continue the interview. That apparently made Margo angry, so she gave a final whine and left the table.

I asked Ms. Landers a few more questions — most of them were absurd, we both agreed — but Ms. Landers graciously answered them all. Then I left.

The next day, Ms. Landers visited the newspaper. Again, she was very gracious. She even told my editors that she thought I was probably a very good night police reporter.

Monday, March 21, 1983.

The North Vietnamese Army likes to attack at night, and with two battalions of the NVA hunkered down in the hills just above my bed (geez, I wished I had set up on the high ground!), you can be sure I slept uneasily Wednesday night.

The first attack came shortly after midnight. I threw off my covers and grabbed my rifle.

Well, actually, I grabbed a bottle of formula and rushed into the children's bedroom. My 8-month-old son, Jack, had started to cry.

In my fantasy world, Jack represented one of the enemy battalions. My daughter, Lorna, represented the other.

When my wife leaves town, which she does for a couple of days each month, I resort to a fantasy life to make my task easier. I pretend I'm a rifle company under siege. When my wife returns — she represents a Marine regiment — I celebrate.

"The reinforcements are here! The siege has lifted!" I shout as she walks in the door.

The children scream, too, happily unaware that in my fantasy world, they represent the enemy.

But back to Wednesday night.

The first battalion came probing my lines shortly after midnight. I had to work quickly, because of the danger that the sound of the attack would wake the second battalion. Especially since the second battalion was sleeping fitfully after a dinner of candy. All that sugar keeps the blood boiling.

"Candy for dinner!" the second battalion had cheered earlier in the evening when Dad had proposed the usual deal.

"If you promise to be a big girl, and play with the

dogs while your dad puts your brother to bed, we'll have candy for dinner. But you must eat all your chocolate-covered peanut butter cups before you get any ice cream. Protein comes first. What do you say?"

"Candy for dinner!" she screamed.

And now she tossed uneasily in her bed while I nursed the first battalion back to sleep.

The second battalion attacked about an hour later.

My daughter, who will turn 4 on Sunday, is at the age in which children begin having nightmares. When the nightmares began a few months ago, it was always about wolves.

"Daddy, there's a wolf in my room," she'd say.

So I spent a lot of time telling her that wolves aren't so bad. Sure, they always play the heavies in fairy tales, but in real life, wolves are nice. They're like dogs.

McClellans like wolves, I told her.

In fact, I spent hours explaining the McClellan philosophy to her. Our ancestors were woodsmen and woodswomen. Wolves and bears and even lions and tigers were our friends.

Lorna is a sharp little kid, and she caught on to the family philosophy. But still the nightmares persisted. They simply changed ever so slightly to fit the family philosophy.

Wednesday night, she woke up screaming.

"Daddy, daddy, there's a lawyer in my room!"

I heard her scream and rushed into the room before her shouts could rouse the first battalion.

"There's no lawyer in here, honey," I said. To calm her fears, I opened the closet. I looked under her bed. No lawyers anywhere.

"Go back to sleep, Lorna, and don't worry. Your dad will stay right here for a while."

Unfortunately, her shouts had stirred the two companies of Viet Cong asleep on the floor. Both dogs began barking.

"Daddy, daddy, there must be a lawyer somewhere. The dogs are barking," Lorna said.

The ruckus woke the first battalion. He stood up in his crib and began howling.

"Jack sees the lawyer, daddy!" Lorna shouted.

Now the battle was raging. The enemy was hitting my lines from all directions.

"Calm down, everybody," I shouted into the din, which only caused the noise level to double, then triple.

"He's going to sue us, Daddy, I know it," my terrifed daughter cried.

I left her and rushed over to take care of the first battalion, which was trying to scale the crib. Often, the best way to calm baby is to change its diaper. Even though Jack's diaper was dry, I began to take it off.

But in the middle of the task, Jack ... Well, let me just say I should have waited a minute.

"Corpsman! I'm hit!" I screamed.

The battle raged for nearly an hour. Finally, the NVA and the Viet Cong ran out of energy, and slipped back into the night.

I returned to bed, exhausted, too tired to sleep.

The next day, my wife returned.

We all cheered as she walked through the door.

"You look terrible," she said to me. "You look like somebody who just ran a marathon."

Wrong fantasy, I said.

Friday, February 26, 1988.

Bless You, Bi-State Buses;
a Spiffier McClellan Is Going Your Way

A couple of weeks ago, I left the newspaper and hustled across the street to the parking lot. I climbed into my car and made all the little checks a prudent person makes before hitting the street.

Was my seat belt on? Check. Did I have a quarter in case I had to park at a meter? Check.

So I zipped out of the lot. I'm too cheap to have a radio in my car, and I'm too concerned with safety to have a telephone in my car, so I normally spend a lot of time looking around.

On this particular day, I happened to look around and see the back of a Bi-State bus.

I saw myself. Sort of. It was like looking in a funhouse mirror. The real me, the one in my car, was a normal guy. The fake me, the one on the back of the bus, was neat and clean and devilishly handsome.

I glanced at myself in the mirror. Then I looked again at my picture on the bus.

It could have been an ad for a miracle drug. Before and after.

What it was, of course, was an advertisement for this newspaper.

At any rate, I did what any normal citizen would do if he were to see a flattering picture of himself on the back of a bus. I spent the rest of the afternoon following the bus.

Once, I pulled even with the bus and honked until the riders looked out at me. Then I waved.

None of the riders made the connection.

I stopped long enough to go home and have dinner with my family.

Even on nights when I've got to go back out, I

usually stick around long enough to read to the kids. But not this night.

"Got to run," I said.

I drove back downtown and prowled around, looking for another bus.

I saw one going the other way. I made a quick U-turn and caught up to it. There was an ad for a radio station on the back of this bus.

Finally, I found what I was looking for. I followed myself around for a couple of hours.

That night I slept fitfully, and the next morning I was back on the prowl. All day I followed myself around.

Regular readers know that I'm not an egotistical person. Oh sure, when I'm at aldermanic meetings or crime scenes or press conferences, I always wait until the television lights go on, and then I walk behind the television reporters so I'll be on the evening news.

But that's a little thing. It only takes a minute, and it doesn't prevent me from writing my newspaper stories.

Following buses, on the other hand, is a full-time job. You can't write a newspaper story while you're following a bus.

So I missed a couple of deadlines.

The bosses put a note in the paper that I was on vacation.

My wife saw the note in the paper and demanded that we go on vacation.

So we packed our suitcases, put the kids in the car and spent a couple of hours following buses around.

"This isn't any fun," my daughter said.

"Watch this. Your dad is going to pull up next to this bus and honk. Get ready to wave!" I said.

But my efforts to include the kids in the fun didn't seem to work.

Finally, they started to cry.

So I agreed to take them on a real vacation.

"Promise us you won't do anything foolish this time," my wife said.

She has never forgiven me for pleading innocent to speeding in Nebraska, refusing to post a bond and thereby getting jailed, merely because I thought that spending the Fourth of July in jail for a speeding ticket would make a good column.

"No jail this time," I said.

So we flew to Tucson and spent a week with my wife's family. We went to the border town of Nogales, and as soon as we crossed the border, I bought us all sombreros so the merchants would know that we were serious about buying trinkets.

Then we went to Phoenix and spent a couple of days with some old friends. Then we flew to Disneyland.

That turned out to be the highlight of the trip. While we were in Disneyland, a building across the street from the amusement park caught on fire.

My life and kids stayed in the park while I ran across the street.

Sure enough, some television guys came, and when the lights went on, I walked behind the reporters.

There I was, on the 10 o'clock news in Los Angeles!

It was almost like being home.

Except, of course, the buses in Los Angeles weren't worth following.

Friday, January 12, 1990.

Trials of a Sensitive, New Age Kind of Guy

As is the case in most modern families, my wife and I split the chores.

For every task assigned to her, there is a task assigned to me. For instance, she does the laundry. I serve as liaison between the household and the government.

That makes sense. As a reporter, I've developed a certain expertise in dealing with officials. It's only logical that I handle all our government-related stuff.

One of my jobs as governmental liaison involves our cars. When it's time to register the cars, the job falls to me.

"My plates are about to expire. You've got to do something about it," my wife said one day last fall.

I told her not to worry. I deal with the police a lot. Consequently, I know a lot of inside stuff.

"You get half a month's leeway," I explained. "Most citizens don't realize it, but when your plates expire in November, you won't get a ticket until the 15th of December."

On the third day of December, she got a ticket.

"That's the exception that proves the rule," I said. "Besides, it must have been a rookie."

"Hardly a rookie," she said. "He looked ready for retirement. He was about your age."

Although I'm not sensitive about my age, my wife realizes I have passed into the third stage of male aging.

The first stage occurs when a guy starts reading about baseball players his own age getting traded because their teams want "to go with youth." That can happen as early as 27.

The second stage comes when cops start looking a lot younger than you do. That happens when a guy hits his 30s.

The third stage — the one I've recently hit — is when you realize that, had you stayed in the army, you could now be living on a pension.

"I could be retired!" is something I say a lot these days.

At any rate, the next day my wife went to the state office on Kingshighway and got her new plates.

Even though she has little experience in dealing with government officials, she had no problems.

"I thought you said it's a big deal," she said haughtily.

"I never said it was a big deal. I said it's a lot more difficult than doing the laundry."

Besides, by then I had a new task.

"Here's my ticket. Don't forget to pay my fine," she said.

I told her I would, but I had a different strategy in mind. Most citizens figure the best thing to do when you're guilty of a traffic offense is to plead guilty, but I make a living covering courts, and I understand that it's possible to beat a ticket.

Admittedly, you need a little luck.

In this instance, I knew I could win only if the cop didn't show up for trial. But what the heck. You can't win if you don't play.

So I went to traffic court, pleaded not guilty on behalf of my wife and was given a date for trial.

Maybe the cop will forget to show, I thought.

Well, life is strange. It was me who forgot to show.

So one day I got a frantic call from my wife.

"Let me read you this letter I got from the city," she said.

Then she started to read:

"Effective immediately, police officers will attempt to arrest you at your residence or place of employment in regard to violations for which you have failed to appear in court. If these attempts are not successful, your vehicle will be towed and held, pending your arrest."

I told her not to worry.

"That's a form letter, honey. It doesn't really mean they'll come looking for you."

"You don't seem to understand," she said. "It's a mistake. They have the wrong person. I've had only one ticket in my life, and you paid my fine, remember?"

"Not exactly," I said. "It sounds like you've missed your court date."

There was a long silence on the phone. Finally, she spoke again.

"You're saying I missed a court date?"

"I'm not saying that, honey. The city is saying it."

Then I told her not to worry. I told her I deal with bondsmen all the time.

"If you should get arrested, and the judge sets a bond of, oh, let's say $10,000, that doesn't mean you really have to pay that much," I started to explain.

"I have no intention of dealing with a bondsman," she said.

Of course not, I assured her. Bondsmen are part of the criminal justice system, and therefore, any dealings between our household and bondsmen would fall to the government liaison. Which is, of course, me.

That wasn't what she meant, she said. She was going to pay her fine.

That's my job, I reminded her.

Well, it turns out that it used to be my job. Nowadays, I do the laundry.

Monday, January 29, 1990.

One of the editors came to work the other day carrying a log.

This is the sort of behavior that newspapers traditionally have tolerated. You can be a little bit off-center, and nobody will make a big deal out of it. "That's a nice log," I said, when I ran across the editor at the coffee machine.

"Do you get it?" he asked, as if the log were some kind of message.

"Sure, I get it," I said.

Actually, I didn't get it, but that's another behavior trait that newspapers traditionally have tolerated. You can act a lot smarter than everybody knows you are, and nobody will make a big deal out of it.

It turns out — maybe you already knew — that the log has something to do with the television show "Twin Peaks."

That's a show I have never seen, but as the editor walked around with the log, it was apparent that a lot of people have watched the show and, therefore, understood the meaning of the log.

From what people tell me, "Twin Peaks" is a very good show.

All the more reason not to watch it, as far as I'm concerned.

I'd get hooked.

I used to watch a lot of television. Back in the days when I was a college student, I used to do two things — watch television and play board games. Monopoly was a favorite. So was Risk.

But mostly, it was television. Soaps in the day, action stuff at night. I used to tell people that my hobby was staring.

Naturally, my grades suffered. I remember the day my adviser gave me a lecture. I tried to listen to what he was saying, but I was distracted. He looked so much like Scottie on General Hospital that I kept wanting to tell him that his wife, Laura, was in love with Luke.

"Your grades are bad," he said.

"Bad grades I can handle," I said. "It isn't as if I'm married and my wife is in love with somebody else."

"Either your grades improve, or you're going to have to find a job where you can act a lot smarter than everybody knows you are," he said.

"I'll find something," I said.

"Good luck," he said.

"Beam me up, Scottie," I said.

That's the kind of joke in which I used to delight. Because my adviser looked like Scottie from General Hospital, I'd make a reference to Scottie from Star Trek.

You really had to know television to keep up with me.

Not many people could and, frankly, not many people wanted to. Except for my Monopoly and Risk friends, my other friends were all too involved with their studies to spend much time in front of the television.

But that was fine with me. If you watch a lot of television, you have a lot of fantasy friends. It was as if I knew all the characters on all the shows.

Oh, they led exciting lives. It saddened me that my life was so dull compared to the lives of the television characters.

Even Lassie, a dog, did more in half an hour than I had done in my entire life.

Sometimes I wondered why I never, not once,

stumbled into an adventure while all the people I knew — the fantasy people — stumbled into adventures all the time.

Then I realized that all the television characters had one thing in common.

They never watched television!

So I quit watching.

Well, I didn't quit all the way. Even today, I watch reruns of Barney Miller, and I always catch, for old times' sake, the "return" shows. "Return to Mayberry," "Dobie Gillis Returns," and so on and so forth.

I like to say that I'll watch anybody return to anywhere.

So while I've never really quit, I have cut way back.

Strangely enough, my life didn't get more exciting when I quit watching so much television.

On the other hand, by the time I quit watching so much television, I was too old to crave excitement. It turns out I had wasted my youth.

Or maybe I had saved myself. Maybe I would have done exciting and foolish things if I hadn't spent my youth parked in front of a television, and maybe I would have gone too far.

Certainly, I would have gotten better grades, and maybe I would have become a doctor or a businessman. Maybe I'd have a secretary, and maybe I'd get stock options and all those good things.

On the other hand, I did find a trade where people can carry logs around and where a guy can act smarter than everybody knows he is.

In a way, then, Scottie did beam me up.

Monday, May 28, 1990.

S aturday morning, and the children were already watching cartoons. I fixed some coffee and threw open the back door to let the dogs out. The fat dog slipped on the ice and ended up on her back, like a bug. As she tried to right herself, I stood at the top of the stairs laughing. My laughter att racted the kids.

"Look at Tia," I said. "Hahahaha."

Finally, she righted herself and threw me a hateful glance.

After letting the dogs back in, I decided to get the paper. I thought briefly about putting on my clothes, or at least my shoes, but decided not to bother. After all, I was wearing my robe.

Out the front door I went.

No wonder Tia had slipped. A sheet of ice was covering everything.

Gingerly, I made my way down the steps. Gingerly, I crossed the lawn, and very carefully I went down the small incline that leads to the sidewalk.

I picked up the paper and headed back.

But I couldn't get back up the mountain.

At least that's what the incline seemed like. It's only about three feet, and it never seemed particularly steep before, but I couldn't get back up.

Meanwhile, my bare feet were beginning to get very cold.

Again, I tried to get up the incline, and again, I slipped back. My feet were now very cold, too cold. I sat down on the ice-covered sidewalk, and rubbed my feet.

I gave myself a pep talk and tried again to get up the incline. One step up, and then I slid back down.

If Jack London had ever written a script for Chevy Chase, this would have been it.

When I looked up at the window — if only my wife were aware of what was happening — the only face that was visible belonged to Tia. She was sitting on the couch, watching me. She loves to sit on the couch and look outside. As far as she's concerned, it's exercise.

Perhaps the cold was beginning to get to me, but it looked as if she were laughing.

She was laughing!

No, she wasn't. It was another face that was laughing. Two other faces. The children!

I hugged myself to pantomime that I was cold. I sat on the sidewalk and rubbed my feet. I hugged myself again.

Now the children were applauding!

In a sense, this was my fault. Several days earlier, the children had complained about the cold, and to show them what a He-Man their father is, I ran outside without a shirt on. I danced around in the cold while they stood at the window cheering.

Obviously, that had been a bad idea. Now, in my moment of need, the kids thought I was trying to amuse them.

I was beginning to get very, very cold.

Desperation led to an idea. If I were to take my robe off, and use it as a carpet, perhaps I could get up the incline.

But if I were to take off my robe, I'd be really cold.

Furthermore, I'd be opening myself to a criminal charge. After all, I'd be exposing myself.

And what if I were to slip, and knock myself out? Without my robe on, I'd be a goner in minutes.

Then I'd really be in trouble. I know a lot of prosecutors, and I know how they work. In my mind, I heard the closing argument in the case against me.

"He's charged with exposing himself. And what does the death certificate say he died from? Exposure!"

I'd be charged with the same thing that killed me. I wouldn't have a chance.

I didn't want to put my family through that ordeal. I struggled to my feet again and took a step up the hill. Back down I slid.

I glanced back up at the window, and wonder of wonders, the children's laughter had awakened my wife. I was saved!

But wait. A closer look revealed that something was wrong. My wife was crying.

I stared at the window. She was crying because she was laughing so hard. Obviously, she didn't know how desperate my situation was.

I hugged myself.

She applauded!

I sat back down on the sidewalk to rub my feet. Moments later, my wife came out. She was wearing her coat, and her boots, and she was carrying towels.

From the top of the incline, she threw me the towels, and I managed to crawl up the hill.

I walked into the house, and the children applauded.

"Good show!" said my daughter.

"Funny!" said my son.

Tia, who looked vaguely disappointed, rolled over and went to sleep.

Monday, January 7, 1991.

Philosopher's Approach
to Valentine's Day

According to my philosophy, Valentine's Day is one holiday that should change with the years. In the days of courtship, chocolates and roses are appropriate. In the early days of marriage, romantic gifts should give way to practical gifts. Roses will wilt in days, but a new coffee pot will last for months.

Finally, when your marriage reaches a stage where the house is filled with dogs and cats and children, and you and your wife are always busy with work and ferrying children to one thing and then another, the very best gift a husband can give is not a gift at all. Instead, he should do something around the house that he has been meaning to do, but has not found time to do.

Like take care of the Christmas tree.

For weeks, it had been a stain on the McClellans' reputation. In a neighborhood that is generally well-kept, our Christmas tree lay like a corpse at the base of our front steps.

Part of my philosophy involves sharing household chores. So it is that all Christmas tree-related tasks are divided in our house. My wife, with input from the children, picks it out at the lot. I drag it to the car. I drag it into the house. My wife is in charge of decorating it.

After the holidays, she's in charge of stripping it of its ornaments. She's in charge of putting the ornaments away.

She did those jobs in early January.

"Now it's your turn to do something," she said. "Get the tree out of here."

I dragged it out the front door. I dragged it to the edge of the steps. I pulled it upright like it was the flag at Mount Suribachi on Iwo Jima.

Then I gave it a gentle shove.

With a glow of self-satisfaction, I went back into the house, and made myself a drink.

"I thought you were going to take care of the tree," said my wife.

"You thought correctly," I said.

"I don't just throw the ornaments into the basement. I put them away," my wife said.

I tried to explain that sharing of tasks only works when each party does his or her assigned task and refrains from criticizing the work of the other.

"You can't just leave the tree at the bottom of the steps," she said.

"That's only a temporary resting stop. I intend to haul it to the recycling center at Forest Park," I said.

That is exactly what I intended to do.

But whenever I decided to act on my intentions, something came up. That's the way life is when the house is filled with dogs and cats and children. Finally, the tree recycling center shut down.

When I realized that this option had been foreclosed, I thought about dragging the tree, in the dead of night, over to my neighbor's lawn. After all, the wind eventually blows my leaves onto his lawn, and he never complains.

So when my wife suggested that the tree was becoming an embarrassment, I gave her a wink.

"I think it's going to be Tom's problem soon," I said. "Strong wind coming tonight."

This is another part of my philosophy. Make a good situation out of a bad situation. A lot of fellows like me, klutzy fellows who can't hammer a nail, would be devastated with a neighbor like Tom.

When he first bought the house, the floors sloped heavily to one side.

"Real smart guy," I said to my wife. "Must not have noticed that the house tilts. Ha-ha-ha!"

It turns out he had noticed. He rented some sort of huge jack, propped up his house, cut something away in the basement and lowered his house until the floors were even.

I could have understood the engineering principle involved in jacking up the house, and then stuffing old magazines under the end that was lower, thereby raising the lower end. But lowering the higher end?

Preposterous.

But it worked. Then he installed his own central air conditioning.

"You're not going to drag the tree over to Tom's lawn," my wife said. "It's bad enough that he ends up raking our leaves."

I tried to explain that Tom probably would be grateful if a Christmas tree blew onto his lawn. He'd probably use the wood to build a deck.

Absolutely not, said my wife.

Fine, I said. Part of my philosphy involves avoiding all arguments. Nobody ever really wins an argument, I like to say.

So the tree continued to rest at the bottom of the steps. January turned to February, and the tree remained.

But finally, with Valentine's Day approaching, and my wife complaining more and more about having to step over the tree every time she comes or goes, I decided to do something. I dragged the tree to the side of the house.

I know it's not exactly what my wife had in mind, but Valentine's Day isn't exactly a major holiday. Besides, my wife's birthday is just a couple of months away.

Friday, February 12, 1993.

Trying to Fathom One Man's Mind: It's a Clothes Call

For the early years of our marriage, my wife was not allowed to throw out any of my clothes.

Then we went to a "Don't Ask, Don't Tell, Don't Pursue" policy. I only hope it works better for the military and homosexuals than it has for me and my clothes.

Although the phenomenon has been underreported, husbands' clothes have become a major source of friction in many contemporary marriages. This is because so many women have become more successful than their husbands, and a successful woman believes that her husband's attire is a direct reflection on her taste.

For instance, Hillary Clinton was probably aghast at the bright pink shirt her husband wore during his visit to St. Louis this weekend.

You see, pink used to be a "power color." That's probably why Hillary bought it for her husband in the first place. By the time pink was again unfashionable, Hillary's husband had grown fond of the shirt. Even though Hillary would no longer let him wear it, he refused to throw it out. Then, as soon as he slipped away from his wife for the weekend, he put it on.

He was rebelling against his wife, who is, of course, more successful than he is.

This sort of rebellion, which is becoming increasingly commonplace, is why so many wives are demanding the right to throw away their husbands' clothes.

Like Hillary's husband, I am married to a successful woman. For years, I resisted her entreaties to periodically purge my closet.

I should take a minute here to briefly explain my relationship with my clothes.

I have always believed that a man should think of

his shirts the way a baseball manager thinks of his pitching staff. That is, you need four, maybe five, starters. A "starting shirt" is a shirt you put on in the morning and wear to work.

In addition, I have always taken a certain pride in the fact that most of my starters are capable of going nine innings. In other words, I'm not one of those Fancy Dans who changes clothes two or three times a day. What I put on in the morning is generally what I wear until I go to bed.

At times, of course, this has resulted in what some people would call inappropriate attire.

For instance, one of my neighbors recently confessed that he was confused when he first moved into the house next to mine.

"I think it was my first or second night in the house, and it was pouring rain; and I glanced out my window and saw you on your roof cleaning the gutters. A flash of lightning illuminated you, and I noticed you were wearing a shirt and tie. 'What kind of neighborhood is this' I wondered, 'where people dress up to clean their gutters?' "

Let me quickly explain that I would never recommend that anyone clean their gutters during a storm. On the other hand, it is easy to forget about your gutters until there is a storm.

But as to wearing a shirt and tie to clean my gutters, I make no apology.

At any rate, because I wear my "starting shirts" so much, I develop a certain affection for them.

"You need a new shirt," my wife will occasionally say.

"There's no room in the starting rotation for a rookie," I'll say.

And, of course, that's a problem. Men tend to think of their clothes as friends. Women think of clothes as clothes.

For me, the problem reached a boiling point last winter. A faithful coat that had achieved the ultimate status — the article had been dropped and the coat was simply referred to, even by my wife, as Coat — had become torn.

"Coat needs to be thrown out," said my wife.

"Coat has a couple of more years left in him," I said.

Christmas morning, there was a new coat under the tree. I grasped the implications immediately and rushed to the closet. Coat was gone.

"Where is he? What have you done with Coat?"

"He's in the trash," my wife said.

"He's where?"

I rushed out and rescued him.

But then my wife came up with the "Don't Ask, Don't Tell, Don't Pursue" policy. (And I'll bet Hillary developed it, too, which is surely how her husband came up with it for the military and homosexuals.)

Although the new policy is supposed to be a compromise, I find I have very little authority.

The other morning, I looked in my closet for Yellow Shirt. Admittedly, he's a bit threadbare, but he's been a faithful companion for several years.

"Yellow Shirt's not in the closet," I said to my wife. "Where is he?"

"You're not allowed to ask," she said, "and I'm not allowed to tell."

I rushed toward the kitchen door, and the alley outside.

"You're not allowed to pursue," she reminded me.

I was crushed. My only solace is the knowledge that I'm not alone. I have a feeling that this morning, Hillary's husband has probably gone to his closet.

"Where's Pink Shirt?" he asked.

"You're not allowed to ask, and I'm not allowed to tell," Hillary said.

Monday, July 19, 1993.

Science Fiasco Leaves Egg on Father's Face

S hortly before 7:48 a.m. last Monday, I gathered my family in the kitchen and, with great fanfare, prepared to stand an egg on its end.

As I readied the egg for balancing, I read the following note to the children:" At the autumnal equinox, the sun is equidistant from the north and the south poles of the earth. Furthermore, the plane of the earth's equator and the plane that passes through the center of the sun are on the same line.

"As a result of this, the gravitational pull between the poles and between the sun and the earth is then equal in all directions. These are the reasons an egg will stand on its end."

As regular readers might guess, I didn't understand any of that. But my lack of understanding is the very reason I had decided to stand the egg on its end.

With a few exceptions, my generation, the baby-boomers, doesn't understand science.

Consequently, this country is unable to compete in the international markets. We've become a debtor nation. We have run up huge budget deficits.

If today's children grow up to be as scientifically illiterate as my generation, our economy will continue to deteriorate. Just as the baby-boomers become eligible for Social Security, there won't be any.

Perhaps that would be poetic justice, but for personal reasons, I hope it can be avoided.

Besides, I'm like all fathers. I want to see my children succeed.

"Now, do you understand why Dad is going to be able to balance this egg?" I asked.

"Not really," said my daughter.

I read the note again.

This time, I tried to read it the way judges read legal instructions to a jury. That is, I put an emphasis on every fourth word.

"At the autumnal EQUINOX, the sun is EQUIDISTANT from the north AND the south poles OF the earth..."

Glancing at the kids, I saw they had the blank look of jurors listening to the mumble jumble of jury instructions.

"Why don't you put it in simpler terms?" suggested my wife sarcastically.

She knows just enough about science to be smug with people like me. Her father is a nuclear physicist, and she always did well in the college science classes that were required to get into dental school.

"It has to with gravity," I said, and both kids nodded solemnly. "You've got your sun, you've got your earth, you've got your poles and in about two minutes, everything comes together. Understand?"

The kids nodded again.

Now, of course, it was my turn to feel smug.

I readied my egg, and glanced at the clock in the kitchen.

"It's time," I said.

Very delicately, I balanced the egg. I felt in touch with cosmic forces. In another life, I was probably a geomancer, using my divining rod to advise chieftains.

I let go of the egg. It rolled on to its side.

My wife applauded.

Quickly, I put the egg back on its end. With a light touch, I held my finger on its top, balancing it. I removed my finger, and the egg rolled on to its side.

Maybe I wasn't a geomancer in a previous life.

As the egg rolled on its side yet again, my wife resumed clapping, and my son, sensing that the applause was derisive and was aimed at me, joined in. He is a child who roots for the Cardinals simply because his father roots for the Cubs.

My wife thinks we should encourage this independence, but I know better. It's not independence as much as rebellion. Today the Cardinals, tomorrow drugs.

"It will never stand up while you two are clapping," I said.

Meanwhile, the dogs, apparently hopeful that the egg might roll off the table and belong to them, began circling under the table like miniature land sharks.

My daughter, always faithful to her father, tried to intervene and balance the egg herself. But even with her lighter touch, the egg rolled on to its side the moment she let go of it.

Finally, I glanced at the clock. The equinox had come and gone.

"Your mother's bad vibes disturbed the delicate balance we needed," I announced.

My wife shook her head.

"That stuff about balancing an egg is just an old wives' tale," she said.

I thought about that for a minute. Maybe husbands used to be smarter than they are today.

Sunday, September 29, 1991.

Mom Is Away, So Dad,
the Boy, and Dog Can Play

Moments after my wife and daughter left town Friday afternoon for a 10-day vacation, I took my son aside for a man-to-man talk.

This was difficult for me. My father was from the generation of men that did not believe in talking man-to-man with their sons. In fact, I can recall only two occasions in which my father and I engaged in such a conversation.

The first time was when my mother decided I was old enough to know the"facts of life." So she talked to my father, and then he called me into the kitchen. My mother discreetly left the room.

"Do you know what sex is?" my father asked.

"Yes sir," I replied.

"Fine," said my father. "The only thing I have to tell you, then, is a bit of advice. There are plenty of girls who will let you go to bed with them because it's a way to get you to marry them."

In those gentler times, older readers will recall, a boy who got a girl pregnant was expected to marry her.

Still, my father's words shocked me. The girls I knew didn't even want to go out with me. The notion that there were plenty of girls who might want to marry me — and especially the idea that they would "trick" me into getting them pregnant in order to marry me — seemed fantastic. Where were all these girls?

Our second conversation occurred a few years later as I prepared to go into the service.

Again, my father called me into the kitchen. He told me to sit down. He looked at me closely for a minute. And I knew that my father, who had survived the war in the Pacific, was comparing me with the men he had known. Finally, he shook his head. Still, he had to say something.

"Don't ever volunteer for anything," he said.

As far as man-to-man conversations are concerned, those were it. So I had very little first-hand experience to go on when I called my 7-year-old son into the kitchen.

Because he had never been away from his mother before, I felt a talk was in order. Even though I'm from a much more communicative generation of fathers than was my dad, I wanted to say something terse and dramatic, something that my son would always remember.

"You're going to learn that some real good food comes out of a can," I said.

I paused, dramatically, to let the words sink in.

If I were a man of my father's generation, that would have been it. But I'm from a generation that can't stop talking.

"You ever hear of a fellow named Dinty Moore?" I asked. Jack shook his head.

"How about Chef Boyardee?" Again, he shook his head.

So I explained that we were going to be "batching it" for the next 10 days,and while a competent bachelor knows how to cook, it is not something he does on a daily basis.

"It's like cleaning the house, Jack," I said. "We will clean the house before your mother and sister return, but we will not be cleaning it on a daily basis."

To get him in the proper mood, I put on an old Tom Waits record. The singer's scratchy voice crooned out the anthem of bachelors.

"And me, I'm sleeping until the crack of noon, midnights howling at the moon. I'm going out when I want to, and I'm coming home when I please. I never need permission, if I want to go fishin', and I never have to ask for the keys."

Jack listened intently.

Then we went to the grocery store and loaded up on bachelor food. Allowed to choose his own cereal, Jack chose stuff that looked very much like candy.

"I'll have to try some of that," I said.

We returned home and settled in for our first night.

"You feel like eating in front of the television?" I asked. "I'll heat up some beef stew and bring it in."

I brought in two bowls of beef stew, two glasses of chocolate milk and two spoons.

"You forgot napkins, Dad," my son said.

"What do you think your sleeves are for?" I asked.

Jack didn't finish his beef stew — "I need to leave room for ice cream," he said — and the dog, sensing that the rules had changed, began whining anxiously.

"No need to save the leftovers," I said. "Let's give it to Jorge."

I carried Jack's leftover stew into the kitchen and ladled it into the dog's dish.

Then I got a couple of blankets and pillows from the bedroom and carried them into the back room. Jack, the dog and I snuggled in to watch television.

Every now and then, the cat came to the door of the back room and looked in disapprovingly.

The cat's attitude was not surprising. Being a female, she couldn't really understand.

Monday, November 21, 1994.

There was an instance, about 10 years ago, when I planned ahead.

As people who know me will attest, that is not usually my style. I prefer to bounce along in life, armed only with a vague belief in karma. If I am nice, perhaps nice things will happen to me. Then again, perhaps not.

When it comes to philosophy, I was Gump before Gump was cool.

So it was very uncharacteristic for me to plan ahead. But I did. I bought Girl Scout cookies.

At the time, my daughter was a toddler.

You can imagine my thought process when I was approached by a woman at the office.

"My daughter is selling Girl Scout cookies," she said apologetically. "I wondered if you might want to buy a box."

I started to say, "No, I believe in instant gratification, and if I have the urge for cookies, I buy them right now, and I eat them right now. Why would I order cookies?"

But I stopped myself.

I realized that for years and years, I had been approached by desperate parents trying to sell Girl Scout cookies. Now that I had a daughter, there was a likelihood that I would someday be in the shoes of the desperate parents.

"I'll have two boxes," I said.

Then I sought out all the other people at the office who were selling Girl Scout cookies.

"I'd like to buy some cookies from you," I said to each of them.

"You don't understand, Bill. You won't get these cookies for several weeks," they said.

"That's all right," I said. "I'm planning ahead."

For the next several years, I bought cookies from any parent who was selling them.

Finally, sure enough, my daughter was a Girl Scout. When it came time to sell cookies, I went with her as she went door to door in our neighborhood. It so happens that there are a lot of children in our neighborhood, and many of the girls are Girl Scouts.

Consequently, most of the people who buy cookies tend to buy one box from each child who comes by. In other words, it is very difficult to sell a lot of cookies.

In the good old days, I suppose, the young saleswomen would just wander farther and farther from home. But parents don't trust the world these days, and that probably explains why so many parents have taken to selling Girl Scout cookies themselves.

It's so much safer.

As I dutifully carried my cookie-order sheet to work, I felt smug about having planned ahead. All the people I had bought from in previous years would be obligated to buy from me. There is, after all, a certain code of honor among parents.

That knowledge sustained me. Under normal circumstances, I would be a terrible salesman. I just hate it when people turn me down. Even as a youth,when I was struggling to get dates, I hated to ask girls out. What if they turned me down?

"One for 10 is better than 0 for 0," went the hustler's creed, but I preferred going 0 for 0.

At any rate, I took my order sheet to work. The people I had bought from did the honorable thing, and ordered cookies from me.

I went home a hero. I had sold more than 40 boxes of cookies.

Weeks later, the cookies arrived. I put them in my car and drove to work. Somehow, though, I had lost the list. I couldn't remember who had ordered what.

"The list must be at home," I thought. "I'll look for it tonight."

On my way to an interview that afternoon, I ate a box of thin mints.

That night, I couldn't find the list, and on my way to work the next morning, I ate another box of thin mints.

Pretty soon, I had eaten most of the thin mints, and I had started working my way through the Samoas.

I knew then, of course, that it no longer made any sense to continue looking for the list. It was no longer possible to deliver exact orders since I had eaten, or was in the process of eating, most of the more popular brands.

Fortunately, nobody complained. That wasn't surprising. Most of the people who had bought cookies from me had done so only out of a sense of obligation, and when I didn't come around to deliver, it also meant that I wasn't coming around to collect.

So I paid for the cookies myself, and I didn't let my wife or children know about my secret life — how I was eating cookies whenever I was in the car, and how I was skipping lunch and eating cookies instead.

Still, I could tell they were suspicious.

As a family, we had ordered a number of boxes, and I noticed my wife looking at me strangely whenever I declined an after-dinner cookie.

Finally, she looked in my car, and discovered what

was left of my cache. I broke down and told her about my secret life.

I am, of course, no longer allowed to sell cookies for my daughter, but this year, one of the younger guys in the office, a fellow with a very young daughter, asked me if I were selling Girl Scout cookies.

"Why do you ask?" I said.

"I'm planning ahead," he replied.

Wednesday, February 15, 1995.

When Dad's Pride Collides with a Coach's Obligation

The runner on second base looked at me expectantly.

"Run on anything!" I shouted. Then, like a seasoned third-base coach, I flashed the signs to the batter.

Of course, the batter wasn't looking at me. In the fifth and sixth grade girls' league, there are no signs. All the kids are supposed to remember is to swing at strikes.

Nevertheless, it keeps me focused to pretend we have signs, so I touched the bill of my cap, clapped twice, dragged my left hand down across my belt, touched my right ear with my right hand, and finally, muttered to myself.

"Please let her hit it," I said.

My 11-year-old daughter was batting.

"You can do it, Lorna!" I shouted.

The pitcher, with "Christ the King" emblazoned on her jersey, zipped the ball toward the plate. Lorna fouled it off.

A feeling of pride coursed through my entire being.

For most of their lives, my children have played soccer. In the Chicago of my youth, we did not play soccer. We considered it an immigrants' game. It was for children who didn't speak English at home.

Now, all the kids play soccer. I don't even understand the rules. But baseball is something I know. I can help my kids with baseball. We've spent hours playing games in our yard and hours more watching games on TV.

My son seems like a natural athlete. He scores goals in his soccer games, and he hits a baseball with surprising authority. But Lorna is very much her father's daughter.

She is more style than substance, athletically speaking. I

used to have wonderful form. I'd knock the dirt off my spikes before stepping to the plate — even when I didn't have spikes. As a pitcher on my Cub Scout team, I'd hold the ball behind my back with my right hand, while my glove hand dangled in front of me, as I stared into the catcher for the sign — even though we didn't have signs.

Until the game actually began, people used to think I was really good.

Lorna has her father's style. She looks good in the batter's box.

Naturally, I was afraid she'd swing and miss. But she didn't. She fouled that first pitch off.

Man, I was on top of the world.

What's more, the team was playing well. We had a chance to win. You can't beat Catholic schools in soccer — that much I know about the game — but apparently baseball does not have the same religious significance, because while we routinely get thrashed in soccer, we were playing these Catholic schoolers dead-even in baseball.

"Way to rip, kid!" I hollered at my daughter, and, to our runner, "Run on anything!"

Lorna fouled the next pitch off.

A great gloom descended upon me. Strike two. I knew what I'd have done in her place. I'd have stepped out of the batter's box, wiped some dirt on my hands, knocked the dirt out of my spikes, and mostly, I'd have tried not to let on that I was thrilled that I'd actually made contact with two straight pitches. No way, I'd know in my heart, would I make contact with the next one.

But Lorna didn't leave the batter's box. She leveled the bat over the plate, and waited for the next delivery. It came, she swung.

Crack!

She hit a roller to the left of the pitcher. The second baseman ran in to pick it up. Our runner from second was streaking into third.

You are almost always safe in our league if you hit a ground ball. Of course, there is always the possibility that the fielder will pick up the ball cleanly, always the possibility that she will make a good throw and always the possibility the first baseman will catch it. But the planets are not often in alignment. Usually, something bad happens.

The second baseman bobbled the ball as Lorna raced down the line. Finally, the second baseman picked up the ball and threw it to first, but the throw was off-line, and the first baseman could only knock it down.

Lorna was safe! With two strikes, she'd come through!

Unfortunately, I had been so obsessed with my daughter's heroics that I had forgotten to send our runner home. Like a good kid, she had stayed patiently at third base, waiting for instructions, as the first baseman kicked the ball around.

I glanced over at head coach Jim Smith, who graciously was pretending to study the score card.

The next batter struck out, and eventually we lost by one run.

"Nobody's fault," I said cheerfully as we trotted off the field, but I knew whose fault it was.

It belonged to the assistant coach who had forgotten to send the runner home. Oh well. He might not be a great third-base coach, but he looked good as he flashed the non-existent signs. Some things never change.

Wednesday, May 10, 1995.

Man vs. Machine: Guess Which Wins?

was driving in St. Charles the other day, bumping slowly along Main Street. The brick street had never seemed so uneven. As I pulled to the curb, I noticed a young man staring at me.

"You are a big deal," I told myself. "Your picture is in the newspaper four times a week, and you are on television every week spouting off about this and that."

Out of the corner of my eye, I saw the young man hesitate as I started to climb out of the car. Obviously, he was trying to work up the nerve to come over and say hello. With some satisfaction — I love attention! — I saw that his desire to meet me had overcome his shyness. He was coming over.

"Hey, Mister. You got a flat tire," he said.

"I'm well aware of that," I said huffily, although, of course, I wasn't. Like most men who are mechanically challenged, I am embarrassed by my ineptitude.

Certainly, a real man — a man who has some feeling for machines — would have known that it was the flat tire, and not the brick street, that had been causing the car to bounce along.

"OK, Mister," said the young man. "Just trying to help."

It was obvious that he knew. He was a guy who understood cars, who could adjust his own brakes, replace his own spark plugs, tell the difference between a carburetor and an alternator, and so on. He had spotted me as one of the Others.

There was a time, years ago, when I drove totally unreliable cars and was forced to learn certain tricks to entice the cars to run. Mostly, though, it was stuff that friends showed me — tap this gizmo with a screwdriver, tighten this thing with a wrench — and I did the tasks with a total lack of understanding.

Mostly, I relied upon superstition. I found, for instance, that if I looked to the left as I turned the ignition key, I had a much higher start-up rate than if I looked straight ahead. Of course, if I looked to the left and the car still didn't start, then no amount of tapping gizmos with screwdrivers would entice the engine to turn over. So it was a gamble.

Despite my ineptitude, I can, of course, change a tire. In fact, I take great pride in doing so. Sometimes I linger over the job, so that passing motorists will see me and note that there is a man changing a tire. He is probably a man who really knows cars, they think. Under normal circumstances, then, I would have been delighted to change my tire right there on Main Street.

Unfortunately, I am not at the top of my game these days. I have pulled a muscle in my back. It is difficult to even sit at my desk and type. The thought of changing a tire made me shudder.

Needless to say, I am not a man who can will himself to ignore pain. So I pulled out my Auto Club of Missouri AAA card. I called for help.

The man who came to my rescue was somewhat older than me. He tried to hide his contempt with cheerfulness. "We'll get you going in a minute," he said.

"Normally, I'd do this myself," I said, trying for a little male bonding. "But I pulled a muscle in my back last week."

"Don't worry," he said. He knew, I thought. "I hate changing my tires myself. I had open-heart surgery six months ago."

"Six months ago," I repeated. " I pulled my muscle last week."

Adding to my feelings of inadequacy was his shirt. He had his first name written above his left pocket.

That is always a sign of a man who knows machines. Repairmen of all sorts have their names on their shirts. It is a status symbol. It doesn't speak of money. It speaks of manliness. I automatically defer to such men. In fact, if I were to sit on some committee entrusted to construct a more perfect union, I would suggest tax breaks for any man whose name is on his shirt. They are the front-line troops, as far as machines are concerned.

The rest of us are Remington Raiders, clerk typists, in the rear with the gear. The guys with their names on their shirts are fighting the battles.

While the older man with his name on his shirt changed my tire, dozens of people passed by. I caught a lot of knowing looks from the men.

Some shot me sympathetic looks. Some didn't try to hide their contempt.

I noticed the young man who had first pointed out the flat tire watching from across the street. He sensed my discomfort and seemed amused by it.

I just wanted to get out of there. When my tire was changed, I climbed into my car and turned the key. The car started. Thank goodness, I thought, I had remembered to look to the left.

Monday, April 28, 1997.

Cubs Going Bust? That's It —
I'm Calling a Lawyer

Like most Americans with even a shred of ambition, I'd really like to sue somebody.

I've always wanted to come up with a good idea and then call Susan Parnell Wilson of Belleville. She is, I figure, a terrific lawyer. At the moment, she's representing Bennie Casson in his lawsuit against PT's Show Club in Sauget.

Casson wandered into the club one night last year only to have exotic dancer Busty Hart allegedly shove her gigantic breasts into his neck and head region. Needless to say, he suffered emotional distress. Wilson figures that ought to be worth $100,000.

That's chump change as far as lawsuits are concerned. But that's what I like about Wilson. She's not a silly lawyer who files frivolous lawsuits demanding ridiculous amounts of money. Obviously, she takes the law seriously. A gigantic breast in the face ought to be worth $50,000. No more, no less. Two gigantic breasts, then, would equate to $100,000.

It's the kind of logic a jury can understand. Especially, I suppose, a Belleville jury.

At any rate, I've been daydreaming about this a lot recently. About lawsuits, that is. Not about gigantic breasts. Why can't I come up with a good case so I can call Wilson?

I was thinking about it as Monday night turned into Tuesday morning. I was in the basement watching the Chicago Cubs lose a 15-inning heartbreaker to the Houston Astros.

As the Cub third baseman picked up what should have been a double-play grounder and fired it wildly into right field, I thought to myself: "Why am I doing this? Why am I spending another entire night watching a last-place team lose again?"

When the answer came to me, I knew I should call Wilson.

I'm addicted.

In their own way, the Cubs are worse than cigarettes. You can smoke a cigarette and still do something else. But watching the Cubs requires full concentration.

Do you know what I was going to do when I first went to the basement Tuesday night?

I was going to work on a book. Instead, I turned on the game. Let's see how the Cubs are doing, I said to myself.

Five hours, 19 minutes, and 15 innings later, I went to bed.

This has happened to me over and over for years. If the Cubs had never been invented, I would probably be a famous best-selling author. Well, maybe I don't have the talent. At the very least, though, I'd be a better newspaper columnist.

Do you realize, for instance, that I was never able — not once — to write anything critical about the Reagan administration? That's because Reagan was once a Cub announcer, and was, therefore, a lifetime Cub fan, and when he said, for instance, that he didn't know what was going on in the White House basement regarding Iran-Contra, I believed him.

Hey, bad things happen. The wind blows out on days when the Cubs are beating the ball into the dirt, and in on days when the Cubs are getting the ball into the air. The third baseman throws a double-play ball into right field. Your subordinates try to give the ayatollah a birthday cake. These things are nobody's fault.

You can't write a good newspaper column with that sort of forgiving attitude.

On the other hand, if it hadn't been for the Cubs, I probably wouldn't be a newspaper columnist at all. I'd have made something of myself. If I had studied the stock market with the same fervor with which I have studied the Cubs — did you know that Lou Brock hit .360 at St. Cloud the year before he came up? — I'd likely be another Warren Buffet.

And we're not just talking about missed opportunities, either. You want to talk about emotional distress?

Ask me about 1984 when the Cubs had to win only one out of three in San Diego to go to the World Series. One out of three.

To this day, I can't stand San Diego, which may be, friends tell me, the nicest city in the country.

I ought to sue. I've got a better case than Casson has.

Don't get me wrong. I'm not trying to play down Casson's emotional distress. I have seen Busty Hart up close.

In 1990, she was arrested for "skipping in a lewd manner" at Busch Stadium, and I interviewed her. She had, I thought then, a good point. Legally speaking, that is. Her argument was this: When you have an 88-inch bust, it's difficult not to skip lewdly.

So sure, if she assaulted Casson, I'm sure he did suffer emotional distress. That ought to be worth $100,000.

But in my case, we're talking real damages. A squandered life and emotional distress.

I'm calling Wilson today.

Wednesday, July 16, 1997.

III

Politics, Women and Business

Day in Court Lets Man Be a Man

Anybody who doesn't believe that women are superior to men ought to spend a day at the courthouse. Any courthouse. Any day.

I happened to be at the St. Louis County Courthouse on Monday morning. I was there for a case involving a basketball hoop.

It seems that in the normally peaceful environs of West County, residents had installed a basketball pole and hoop on the common grounds of a cul-de-sac. Not everybody liked this impromptu park.

My guy, for instance. He objected to it.

One morning, as he backed out of his driveway in his truck, he accidentally rammed the pole. He hit it with such force that the pole and the hoop somehow attached themselves to his truck. He did not realize that he was dragging the pole as he left the cul-de-sac and drove down the street. He only realized that he was dragging something after he had turned the corner. Then he got out of his truck, and did what any good citizen would do. He pushed the pole and hoop off the side of the road.

At least, that was his story. The neighbors thought he had done this thing intentionally.

Perhaps because one of the neighbors happens to be a chief of police for one of our western municipalities, my guy was charged with felony stealing. The trial was supposed to begin Monday morning.

Frankly, I was somewhat skeptical of my guy's story. It sounded to me like he had gotten angry, simmered about it and then had done a guy thing.

While I was in the hallway waiting for his trial to begin, a woman approached me. She had recognized me from the newspaper.

What brings you here? I asked. My husband, she said.

Of course. Unless a woman is a lawyer, a courthouse employee, a juror, or a witness, she's usually at the courthouse for her husband or her son.

In this case, the woman's husband had been busted for DWI.

He was sitting on a bench in the hallway. He had that humble, hang-dog demeanor that guys get when they've done something bad. Might as well wear a sign: "I'm Flawed, but What Did You Expect? I'm a Man."

You'll probably be all right, I told him. Is this your first? My fifth, he said.

Could be prison, I said.

He said he was hoping for work release. He added that he had quit drinking, and was going to meetings a couple of times a week. So he could handle any kind of probation, he assured me. He was never going to drink and drive again.

His wife, who had surely heard that story before, didn't say anything. They have two kids in grammar school, and now her man, who's probably a good and decent man, was turning the world upside down. For a drink.

I went back into the courtroom to see if my guy's case was up yet. It wasn't. The judge was accepting a guilty plea. From a guy, of course.

This fellow looked to be about 35. He, too, had the hang-dog demeanor. He was pleading guilty of having had sex with a 14-year-old. It was consensual, his lawyer later assured me, and the guy had never been in trouble before, but still . . .

The man's wife sat in the second row. She was dressed as if for church, and she did a wonderful job of maintaining her dignity. Expressionless, she watched the proceedings.

Her man, I thought to myself. Her man. With him, it hadn't been booze, but it had been another guy thing.

I went out to feed the meter, but stopped abruptly in the lobby. A car was resting inches from the front door. Somebody had jumped the curb and pulled up to the courthouse door. Undoubtedly, this was another guy thing.

Indeed. The car belonged to a 46-year-old man who had been in court earlier in the morning. He had been representing himself — the male ego at work, he didn't need an attorney — and he had wanted the judge to order the arrest of his ex-wife.

The judge advised him to get a lawyer, so the man decided to make a guy statement. Now he was sitting against the wall, his arms handcuffed behind him. He was wearing a shirt and tie and an expression of righteousness, which so often precedes the more becoming and natural hang-dog look.

After feeding the meter, I went back up to the courtroom to discover that the basketball case had been disposed of. My guy had agreed to donate $500 to the Backstoppers — undoubtedly the chief's favorite charity — and write a letter of apology to the neighborhood children. In return, the charges were dropped.

Not surprisingly, this sensible deal had been arranged by the prosecutor, who happened to be a woman.

As I was leaving the courthouse, I ran into a defense attorney of my acquaintance.

"It's Flawed Guy Day in the courthouse," I said.

"As always," she said, and then she hurried off to meet her client, who was, no doubt, a man.

Wednesday, August 20, 1997.

Woman Befools "Regular Guy"

I f something seems too good to be true, it probably is. Why can't bachelors understand this?

Consider what happened to a fellow who is calling himself Larry. And let me digress here for an instant.

This newspaper recently received a packet of letters. Actually, they were copies of letters. The man who sent us this packet wanted to embarrass a certain woman. However, because the story was also embarrassing to him, he had inked out his own name from these letters and had given himself the pseudonym of Larry. By holding the letters under a light, I was able to detect our hero's real name. But in an instance like this, male solidarity must count for something; so, Larry he shall remain. And now, back to our story.

Larry heard of an outfit called Romantic Pen Pals. For $10, RPP will send you a list of women who are interested in being pen pals. This is a very special list.

Accompanying each woman's name is a photograph and a short biography.

The photographs are, to say the least, revealing. The biographies are as scanty as the clothes.

There are several things that would make a rational man wonder about the legitimacy of the service.

In the first place, the women's names sound a bit phony. My favorite is April May, who hails from the St. Louis area. In the second place, all the addresses are P.O. Boxes.

But most telling, I think, are the descriptions of the kind of men to whom these women are attracted.

Most legitimate such services — I think of the personals in the Riverfront Times, for instance — are rather depressing to a normal guy.

"Attractive female seeks slender, financially secure, professional man who enjoys opera and classical music."

But hey, that's life. That's the kind of man most women think they want until they meet a paunchy, paycheck-to-paycheck guy who enjoys watching sports on television.

The women in RPP have already reached that level of enlightenment. In fact, they're not even that particular. Here's a sample of their wish lists:

"Victoria O'Hara seeks man 21-55."

"Ali Magee needs a man."

"Liz Southern seeks steady guy."

"Pauline Gawron wants to live with a man, 20-65, not fussy."

Bearing in mind that all these women are attractive — and some are extremely attractive — a rational man might wonder how it is that these women, with their sights set so realistically low, have to advertise.

On the other hand, it's probably a kick to realize, "I qualify!"

So it was, apparently, with Larry. He selected an attractive 24-year-old whose mailing address was a post office box in Maryland Heights. Her name, supposedly, was Linda. She had no particular specifications for her dream guy. Her biography just said, "Needs love."

He wrote her a letter.

"I want to give you all the love you desire," he wrote.

He explained that he was quite a bit older than her, but looked 10 years younger than his real age. He said he was 5-foot-8, and weighed 155 pounds.

She responded quickly.

"You write an interesting letter, and you really are a very romantic guy, I can tell," she said. She threw in a couple of very personal asides — as he had in his letter — and then she asked for money.

"You might think about sending some money so I can send a few color photos," she suggested.

Larry sent her $5 with his next letter. He also suggested that they get together. Why write letters when they live so close?

Again, she responded quickly.

"I've never met a man like you before," she wrote. And yes, she wanted to meet him in person. She suggested a motel in Belleville. They could meet in the lounge. But she would need $50 in travel money.

That was fine with Larry. He wrote back to establish a time for the meeting. He did, however, have a question.

"Have you met many men since you placed your ad? I hope I'm your one and only," he wrote.

In her next letter, she assured him he was.

So he sent her $50 and went to the appointed motel at the appointed hour.

Linda did not show up!

Nor did she respond to any more letters, not even the one in which Larry threatened to take his story to the press.

Which, of course, he eventually did. I present it here as a cautionary tale.

Beware, bachelors, of attractive young women who pretend to be enlightened enough to want us normal guys.

Remember, they all think they want slender, financially secure professional men who enjoy opera and classical music.

We regular guys are an acquired taste.

Wednesday, January 6, 1993.

Men Not Suited for Much,
Many Women Think

When Anita Hill galvanized the sisterhood, it was natural and expected that the "anti-Suit" fervor would seep down even to those of us who don't really qualify as Suits. Properly used, the term means a male boss.

But when Hill was getting grilled by the Suits in the Senate, any man who said anything in defense of the senators became a target of opportunity.

Most men were surprised at the intensity of the rage. "They don't like us," we said to each other.

Time passed, and the memory of those times grew dim. In their foolishness, men began thinking again that women like them. And hey, why not? Men are great, and wise and generous. At least, men think so.

Truth is, though, those sentiments are not shared by women. In fact, the anti-man feelings never really went away. They've been surfacing again in the wake of President-elect Clinton's announcement that he would lift the ban on homosexuals serving in the military.

Shortly after Clinton's announcement, I mentioned that I had certain misgivings about the lifting of the ban.

"Gays have always served in the military," I said. "And maybe I'm old-fashioned, but I kind of like the way it used to be. Gays could serve, but they couldn't be open about being gay. That way, there was no problem."

In other words, I don't like the idea of witch-hunts in which military investigators follow people around to determine their sexual preference. I simply think that if your sexual taste runs toward men, it's better if the other guys in the barracks don't know that.

That seems like a reasonable attitude, doesn't it?

You should have seen my mail, and monitored my phone.

"It absolutely amazes me that so many guys think it would be distasteful to have guys hitting on them," wrote one woman. "Ask any attractive woman. Unwelcome advances from men are simply a fact of life, like ants at a picnic."

Like ants at a picnic. They think of us as bugs!

Actually, this theme, and variations on it, were played over and over.

It would serve men right, women said, if gays did make unwelcome sexual advances toward them.

Of course, a lot of women pointed out the obvious — gay men are hardly ever predators. That is, a gay man won't try to force himself on a straight man.

The sexual predators in our society are heterosexual men. So said my callers anyway. And if you think about it, they're absolutely correct.

Which brought up another point.

"All these men talking about not wanting to be somebody's sex object is a joke," a woman friend told me. "What makes most straight men think gay men would be interested in them?"

Gee, I don't know, I said.

"Let me explain then," she said. "Your typical man has a ridiculously high opinion of himself. The typical man thinks he's attractive. That's why you see so many older guys trying to flirt with young women. They don't realize how stupid they look.

"While women are constantly trying to watch their weight, a man can blithely ignore his ever-expanding belly. Sometimes it seems like you guys must have magic mirrors. No matter how awful the truth is, a man somehow thinks that he looks good," she said.

As she talked, I felt rather uncomfortable. Although I happen to be a very good-looking man — the sort of fellow who doesn't look foolish if he innocently flirts with a younger woman — I suppose I could afford to lose three or four pounds.

Another caller asked me if I knew any gay men.

Of course I do, I said. Several of my friends are gay.

Have any of these gay friends ever hit on you? the caller asked.

Of course not, I said. They know I'm straight.

Have you ever made any unwelcome advances on women? the caller asked.

I'm a married man, I said. But in my single days, many of my advances were unsuccessful, so I suppose you could say they were unwelcome.

Then you have no moral right to be concerned about unwelcome advances, she said.

Wait a minute, I said. Every man has made his share of unwelcome advances.

My point exactly, the caller said.

And so it went.

Interestingly, most of the mail and calls were from women rather than from gays. And most of the response had very little to do with the actual subject of gays in the military.

For the most part, the women just wanted to say that men are, by and large, jerks.

Hard to believe, but there it is.

Monday, November 23, 1992.

What's Rat Poison among Friends?

Burt Reynolds starred in a movie called "The Man Who Loved Women." I didn't see the film, but I read a review written by one of my colleagues. Apparently, Reynolds played a sculptor who fell in love with every woman he met and remained in love with his old loves even as he was falling in love with new ones.

What a stale plot! What a waste of an excellent title! Here in St. Louis, we have a man whose story, if it were told on the silver screen, would deserve the title.

His love is so strong that he requested I not put his name in the newspaper.

"I don't want to bring no trouble down on anybody," he said.

I don't like to use pseudonyms. But in this instance, I will. I'll call our hero Burt.

Burt lives on the city's near north side. The house he lives in is a bit raggedy, as is Burt himself. He's almost 60, and on Friday morning, when I visited him, he was unshaven. He was also surprised that I had heard of him. I explained that some cops I know had spoken of him. How did his name come up, he wondered. I said that the cops had been talking about unusual crimes. One of the cases that came up in the conversation was the Shirley Allen case.

Burt grinned.

Shirley Allen is the woman who allegedly spiked her husband's beer with anti-freeze. She was supposed to have done it on a regular basis. Her husband eventually died, and Mrs. Allen was convicted of murder.

Oh, I remember that one, said Burt.

That's not surprising. One of Burt's wives — he's had several — tried a similar thing with Burt. She put rat poison in his coffee. She allegedly did it on a regular basis for about six months. Burt knew something was wrong. He felt sick all the time. His stomach felt as if it were on fire.

"I thought I had an ulcer," he said. "I tried everything. For a while, I drank goat's milk. The only thing that made me feel better was whiskey."

Finally, a relative caught Burt's wife in the act, and she confessed. At last, Burt knew what was wrong. He spent more than a month in City Hospital, where the doctors repaired, as best they could, the damage to his stomach and intestines.

Well, people are always doing horrible things to each other. Rat poison in the coffee would be worth a few stories on cold nights, when the cops are dawdling over reports, trying to gain a few extra minutes of warmth. But Burt's case entered the legendary status when he decided not to prosecute.

"Didn't want to get her in trouble," he said. "Didn't then. Don't now."

She was, Burt explained, 20 years younger than he. And it wasn't hate that led her to the rat poison, it was love.

"She was a jealous little thing," Burt said. "And I'm afraid I gave her reason to be. I drank a lot and ran around. Besides, what good would it do to send her to the penitentiary? I just wanted to get away from her."

Burt is remarried, but he has remained friends with the woman who fed him rat poison. In fact, he has remained friends with her family. Her family, incidentally, was angry with her when they learned what she had been putting in Burt's coffee. Still, Burt and his new wife occasionally get together with his ex-wife and her family.

"Sometimes I'll mention rat posion to her, and she'll just laugh," Burt says of his ex-wife. "I laugh, too, but I'm careful around her. One time we were over at her sister's for dinner, and I wouldn't eat anything because she had helped prepare the food. I wasn't trying to be nasty or anything. I just wouldn't have been able to enjoy the food, knowing that she had been in the kitchen."

While Burt and I were talking, his new wife asked if we wanted coffee. I declined the offer, but Burt accepted.

"She treats me real good," he said of his new wife. "Takes care of me like I was a baby."

She smiled and went into the kitchen. A few minutes later, she put a cup of coffee in front of him.

"You don't feel you should watch her make it, huh?" I asked kiddingly.

Burt laughed and said he wasn't worried. Besides, he added, he used to drink it with cream and sugar, so the color was milky, anyway, and the cream probably disguised some of the taste of the rat poison.

"I drink it black now," he said.

We talked for a few more minutes. I assured Burt I wouldn't use his name or his address.

"It's not me I'm concerned about," he said. "I don't want anybody thinking I'm trying to dredge up a case against my ex-wife. Like I told you, I don't want to get her in trouble."

As I left, I glanced at his cup. The man who loved women had finished his coffee.

Monday, January 14, 1985.

Orchestrating Personal Ads

I f you were to call me and say that you were having trouble meeting a person of the opposite sex, I would transfer you to Martha Carr, a colleague of mine who writes about that kind of thing. She would probably tell you to become active in the community and meet people that way.

If you were to reject that advice — if you become active in the community, you'd meet somebody who's active in the community, and then you'd spend the rest of your life getting dragged to meetings — I'd be sympathetic, but I still wouldn't help you. I'm not in the business of playing Cupid.

But every now and then, along comes a situation in which Cupid needs a shove. Such a situation is unfolding right now.

Leonard Smith is looking for a woman.

On the surface, that's no big deal. Smith is single. He's a healthy 64-year-old man. He knows that love can give meaning to a man's life.

Smith works as a security guard at the Shell Building in downtown St. Louis. That is not a good job for meeting women. Most of the women who go past his station are rushing around on business. Besides, Smith works the 4 to 11 shift, and the building is closed for most of that period.

So Smith is trying another route. He is responding to the personal ads in a free weekly newspaper that circulates downtown.

Maybe you've seen those ads. The ads make it clear that this city is filled with attractive, professional, slim, affectionate, fun-loving women who wish to meet a non-smoker.

Smith smokes a pack of cigarettes a day. He's ineligible to answer most of the ads. And many of the attractive, professional, affectionate women are looking for someone who is, as they say in their ads, financially secure.

Smith does not even own a car.

Still, he persists. He answers the ads that seem most reasonable. He answered two last week.

One was from a "big beautiful woman who has a great deal to offer and just happens to be obese."

Another was from a woman who enjoys baseball games and bowling and is emotionally fit.

Both of those women sounded appealing to Smith. He wrote them each a letter. He explained that he enjoyed flea markets and country and Western music. He said he loved to cook. He described himself as gentle, loving, and caring. He said he drank two cans of beer a day and smoked a pack of cigarettes.

Smith did not pretend to be a matinee idol. He didn't say he was good-looking or well-built. Except for noting his height (5 feet 10), the color of his hair (brown) and the color of his eyes (blue), the only mention he made of his appearance concerned his tattoos. He has 15 tattoos, he said, seven on one arm, eight on the other.

All in all, the letters were straightforward and honest. But as of the middle of this week, neither woman had responded.

Maybe they got the wrong impression from the letters. Maybe they thought Smith sounded dull or unromantic. They probably did not realize that Smith is a man willing to lose everything for love. And he is.

The last time he went looking for love in the classifieds, it cost him his job.

He was working for a security guard company. He was stationed, more or less permanently, at Powell Hall. The year was 1979.

He wrote a personal ad, and the paper published it. It was a straightforward ad. A gentle and caring man wanted to meet a woman. Meet me at the guard station at Powell Hall any night the Symphony is playing, the letter said. It was signed Leonard S.

Unfortunately for Leonard Smith, some women put two and two together and came up with five. They thought that the only caring and gentle Leonard S. at Powell Hall was Leonard Slatkin. He is the conductor of the Symphony.

Perhaps some of those women complained. Perhaps Slatkin complained. It doesn't matter who complained.

What matters is that Smith got fired. Powell Hall is only big enough for one Leonard S.

Before getting fired, though, Smith did meet a woman at the guard station. Her name was Lucille, and she and Smith lived together for four years, until Lucille died two years ago.

So Smith says he is glad he put the ad in. If you believe in love, which Smith obviously does, you know that love is more important than a job.

What a shame that such a romantic attitude did not come through in Smith's letters. If it had, I'm sure at least one of the women would have answered him by now.

I think he could make some woman happy, even though his last name isn't Slatkin.

Friday, August 23, 1985.

Laboring under a Misconception?

C ontemporary women are very good at assuming guilt. Maybe it has something to do with the women's movement and the changing times, but for whatever reason, a woman of the '80s is always willing to feel guilty about something.

Naturally, then, Debbie Chapman has assumed a certain amount of guilt for having had her baby at home. The baby is healthy, so it's no big deal, but Debbie is a registered nurse, and she believes that a prudent woman goes to a hospital to deliver a baby. Hospitals are better prepared to deal with emergency situations, Debbie believes. But a little more than a month ago, Debbie had her baby at home.

"I guess it's really my fault,' she says.

Her husband, Dave, nods sagely when she accepts her guilt. Yes, I can see how it is your fault, he says. You were three weeks early. But perhaps some of the guilt belongs to me.

Oh, he's a magnanimous sort! Willing to assume a little guilt himself. That bothers me. The home birth is certain to become a Chapman family legend. As the years go by and the tale is told and retold, there's no telling how the truth will be distorted. Therefore, as a service to the child, Ryan Keith Chapman, I hereby give the true account of the incident.

Dave is a doctor. On the night of Oct. 22, he went to a dinner that was sponsored by a drug company. Drinks were served before dinner. Dave is a friend of mine, and I can tell you that he does not drink much or often. But he is, after all, a friend of mine, so you can assume that if somebody else is buying the drinks, he'll probably have one or two. Which he did.

He got home shortly before midnight.

Debbie was not in bed. She was walking around. She told Dave she had abdominal cramps. She was convinced she was about to have the baby. She washed her hair, and packed her bag, readying herself for the hospital.

Dave was asleep when she got out of the shower.

She woke him up, and said she was going to have the baby.

"I thought she was nuts,' Dave recalls. "I went back to sleep."

That's the problem with being married to a doctor. A normal man would panic, and rush his wife to the hospital. But doctors always know better than their patients. Get a good night's sleep and see how you feel in the morning. That's what Dave advised Debbie.

A couple of hours later, Debbie woke Dave again. He checked her blood pressure. It was high, so he called her obstetrician, who prescribed some medication. Dave dutifully got up and went out to get the medication. He came back, gave Debbie the medication and went back to sleep.

At about 5:30 a.m., she woke him again. I think I'm about to have the baby, she said.

Dave has the patience of Job, so he roused himself once more. Silly woman, he must have thought. But he got up, and gave her a quick check.

She was about to have the baby! Well, you can imagine how upset he was. Why hadn't she been more persistent? Why wasn't she in the hospital? Why had she let things get so far out of hand?

He didn't panic. Instead, he rushed to the telephone book and looked up "ambulance." He called the company with the biggest advertisement. Then he looked around to see if he had the proper equipment with which to deliver the baby.

He didn't. How could he have known his wife would do this? He had one sterile glove in his bag, and that was it. He grabbed a shoelace and a sewing scissors. He tried to keep his wife calm, and never said a word about how all this was her fault.

Wouldn't you know it? The ambulance had the last two digits of the address wrong. How could that have happened? Dave saw the ambulance rush past his house. He started out the door to stop the ambulance, but Debbie was about to have the baby and she screamed at Dave not to leave. So Dave flicked the lights on and off a few times, and rushed back to Debbie.

He reached down, and felt the baby's head.

Because Debbie was three weeks early, she had not completed her Lamaze course. One of the classes she had not yet had deals with how to push, how to eject the baby. But it turns out Debbie didn't need much in the way of direction. All of a sudden, the baby started to emerge.

The ambulance crew saw the lights go on and off, and they came to the door. We can have her at the hospital in four minutes, one of the crew said. That will be too late, said Dave, and he asked if the crew had a precipitous delivery kit. The crew did, and Dave used it to deliver the baby.

The baby was fine. He checked in at 5:52 a.m., and weighed 5 pounds and 5 ounces. He was 18 inches long. He started crying the moment he was born, and he has scarcely stopped since. Cryin' Ryan, they call him.

And someday, when he hears the story about his birth, I hope he understands whose fault it was. And I'm sure he'll forgive her.

Wednesday, November 28, 1984.

Men Can Stand a Little
Damp in a Warm Cave

I have sometimes been criticized by other men because of my willingness to accept the fact that women are the smarter sex.

Last week, for instance, I wrote a column about secretaries, and I casually mentioned, as I so often do, that women are smarter than men.

A number of fellows called to complain. You never say anything nice about men, they said. Surely, there must be some ways in which we're superior to women, they said.

Those callers had a point.

Men are more in touch with their past.

That thought came to me during the downpour Sunday morning. I was in the basement, watching television, and thoroughly enjoying the notion that I was warm and dry while the first great storm of the spring raged on outside.

That's because I'm a man. I understand what a house is. It's a cave. It's where we've sought shelter for thousands of years.

Women have lost touch with this basic truth.

My wife, for instance, became absolutely agitated when she started down toward the basement and discovered that the steps were damp.

"Water's getting in!" she shouted.

"I haven't noticed," I replied. "It's warm and dry in this section of the cave."

And, really, that's the bottom line, isn't it? Even if your cave isn't completely waterproof — and what cave is? — you should be grateful that large sections stay dry in even the worst of storms. In the old days, guys were always moving the animal skins from the wet sections to the dry sections. It was no big deal.

But women have forgotten. They think it's cause for alarm if even a tiny section of the cave is wet.

"I think the drain outside the back door is clogged," my wife said. "You'd better go out there."

That made no sense. In order to keep the steps from getting wet, I had to get soaked. It's as if I exist to serve the steps instead of the other way around.

Truth is, I get wet almost every time it rains. Like most men, I never remember to clean the gutters until it rains. On a sunny day, it's hard to remember that we even have gutters.

Because the wind was too strong Sunday to risk a trip on to the roof, I figured I was destined to stay dry. Suddenly, though, I was being asked to go unclog the drain.

I went outside, scraped the leaves away from the drain and then poked a coat-hanger into the little holes until the problem was fixed. The water was soon flowing away from the door and into the drain.

In a sense, I felt pretty good about it. Although I come from a long line of handy men, I am not handy myself. I cannot always remember which way to turn the screw to tighten something, for example. Consequently, I seldom fix anything, and when I do, I feel an inordinate sense of satisfaction.

So sure, I stayed outside a little longer than I really had to. Even after the drain was cleared, I remained crouched down, poking at it. I was hoping, of course, that the neighbors might see me.

"McClellan is outside fixing something. I never realized he was handy."

Finally, I went back inside.

"Dad, you're soaked!" said one of the kids.

"Your father had to get the leaves away from the drain," said my wife, and there was something almost accusatory in her tone, I thought, as if the failure to pick up the leaves last fall — it was supposed to be my job — was the real cause of my present condition.

"It was a little more complicated than scraping a few leaves away," I said. "The drain was clogged, and rather than try to get a plumber out here in this weather, I decided to fix it myself."

My wife shook her head, and instructed me to take a shower. It is, of course, another oddity of female-think to consider the cure for a soaking to be a shower.

At any rate, I took a shower and changed my clothes and went back to the basement to watch television.

My wife, meanwhile, prowled around the basement. Touching this corner, touching that corner, going back to the steps to check for dampness.

Naturally, I said nothing, but I kept thinking about the past that I am so in touch with. I thought of the countless caves my ancestors have lived in, and how grateful they must have been if one of those caves was 99 percent waterproof.

Why can't women understand the concept?

After a while, the winds died down, and rain began to slacken.

"I think it's safe to get on the roof and clean the gutters," my wife said.

Reluctantly, I prepared to leave the cave again.

Monday, April 29, 1996.

Candidate's Record: Courting Trouble

Two thousand, eight hundred and 14 people voted for Paul Binggeli this year in the Republican gubernatorial primary.

That's a lot of people. Of course, Paul finished well behind John Ashcroft and Gene McNary, but those two candidates had campaign organizations and plenty of money. Paul didn't have either. So voters didn't have much opportunity to hear Paul's thoughts on the issues of the day.

Truth is, Paul didn't have much to say about most of the issues, and he had virtually nothing to say about the only issue that was hotly debated in the Republican primary. That issue, you remember, was desegregation, and the debate was limited to discussions about which candidate was most opposed to it and which candidate was willing to spend the most public money to prevent it.

Paul had only one issue. He wanted to reform the judicial system. He had selfish reasons for wanting to do that. He wanted to impeach a couple of judges.

I figured that was a splendid reason to want to be governor. I still haven't figured out why all the other candidates in both parties were willing to raise and spend millions of dollars in order to get a job that pays $60,000 a year. Either they know something about the job that the rest of us don't, or else they're too ambitious to be trusted. Paul seemed to be the only candidate whose candidacy was rooted in logic. He wanted to get even.

Paul and I talked often during the primary campaign. I told him I couldn't write about his quest without making him seem like a nut. But maybe I can do something when the election is over, I said.

So Paul put me on his mailing list, and for the last few months, I have been able to count on getting at least one letter a week. Many of the letters have been carbon copies of letters he has written to various newspapers. As far as I have been able to learn, none has been published. That might be because Paul says exactly what he thinks, and what he thinks is usually libelous.

That's why a Ray County associate circuit judge filed a $525,000 lawsuit against Paul and a small Ray County newspaper in 1980 when Paul made his first bid for the governor's job. The judge objected to a paid political ad that Paul placed in the Lawson Review. At the time, the paper had a circulation of 1,100. Paul's advertisement was highly criticial of the judge.

The judge had put Paul in jail for allegedly writing a threatening letter. Paul contended that the letter was not threatening, just nasty. He also contended that his right of free speech was being impinged on. So Paul wrote a letter from the Ray County jail.

I have a copy of that letter, and it is a thing of beauty. He quotes Thomas Jefferson and the Apostle Paul. No newspaper would publish it, but Paul kept it anyway. It's titled, "In the Jailhouse Now." For legal reasons, I can't print it. But I can tell you a little about Paul Binggeli and his ongoing feud with the system.

Paul was a combat soldier in World War II. He married after the war, and he and his wife had one child, a daughter, who is now 21 years old. She is a Down's syndrome child. Paul and his wife took care of the child in their home. Then Paul's wife died in 1975.

From all accounts, Paul, who was working, had a difficult time caring for his daughter. So the state decided — actually, as Paul would point out, a judge made the decision — that the child would be better off as a ward of the state. No one accused Paul of abusing his daughter. No one said he didn't love her. In fact, part of the evidence against Paul would seem to indicate that perhaps he loved her too much. One of the things he was accused of was over-feeding his daughter.

'She loves spaghetti,' Paul told me. 'I used to make a huge pot of it, and she'd eat and eat.'

A nutritionist would certainly tell you that overeating is not good for a child. Paul admits he knew that, but he says that eating is something his daughter enjoys, and there are too few things she can enjoy, so he let her eat as much as she wanted.

The state took her away. It was in the child's best interests, the state said, and the caseworker with whom I talked agreed with the state's decision. The person who was given custody of the child believed that Paul's visits only upset the child, so Paul lost his visitation rights.

He hired a lawyer to fight the state, and that fight has dragged on and on. Paul wanted his daughter transferred to a group home in Kansas City so he would be able to visit her whenever he wished. He also wanted to impeach all the judges who had ruled against him.

Paul won half his fight. On Nov. 26, his daughter was transferred to a group home, and Paul's visitation rights were restored. He never got to exercise those rights, though.

Paul Binggeli died of a heart attack on Nov. 27.

Wednesday, December 5, 1984.

Quayle, Evel Land Safely

Twenty-three years ago, Evel Knievel became famous by breaking nearly every bone in his body when he tried to jump his motorcycle over the fountains at Caesars Palace in Las Vegas.

Several years later, long after he had recovered from his terrible injuries, he announced his intention to set a "world's record" by jumping his motorcycle over 24 trucks. "More dangerous than the Caesars Palace jump!"

That's the way it was billed.

Naturally, I went.

There were a couple of warm-up acts. A stunt pilot flew high over a field near the stadium, and then went into a stall. The plane plummeted toward the ground. Suddenly, just moments before the expected crash, the engine roared to life, and the plane leveled off.

The crowd booed.

The next act was a parachute team. Down, down, down they fell.

After seemingly waiting a moment too long, the chutes opened, and the daredevils floated safely to earth.

The crowd booed.

Then Knievel appeared. He did a few wheelies, made a couple of false starts toward the row of trucks, and then, finally, he raced along the ramp in front of the trucks.

Up, up, up and over.

The spectators just sat there. It's hard to justify booing when you've just witnessed a world's record, but still, we had come to watch a crash.

After all, Knievel didn't become famous by successfully jumping over things.

I was reminded of all this when Vice President Dan

Quayle came to St. Louis on Tuesday to speak at a fund raiser for H.C. Milford, the county executive.

"More dangerous than the speech for the United Negro College Fund!"

That's the way it should have been billed. For Quayle aficionados, that speech was the vice president's finest moment.

"It's a terrible waste not to have a mind," he told the audience.

When the crowd gathered at the Adam's Mark on Tuesday, the whole thing reminded me of the Evel Knievel performance of so many years ago.

After all, Quayle didn't become famous by successfully delivering his speeches.

At Tuesday's show, there was only one warm-up act.

That task fell to the country's most boring governor, Missouri's own John Ashcroft.

After years of speech-making, Ashcroft understands that it's best to start a speech with a funny story.

His funny story had to do with the fact that he and his wife had been traveling. They had to get up early Tuesday morning.

"So Janet says to me, 'John, we got up before the sun got up today.' And I say, 'Janet, you're wrong.' "

And then he paused, so the rest of us could tell that the punch line was coming.

"Then I say, 'We didn't get up before the sun got up. We got up before the sun even thought of getting up!' "

What a fine storyteller the governor is.

After starting his speech with such a bang, he gave the Republican faithful a pep talk, and then he announced that the next speaker was a man "who has fought and overcome the odds."

That made me think there was going to be a second warm-up act, but it turns out he was referring to Quayle.

As the vice president walked to the podium, I thought of Knievel racing along the ramp.

He hit the top of the ramp and flew skyward.

Quayle praised the president for the way he's handled the crisis in the Persian Gulf. He talked about the importance of electing Republicans to the United States Senate. He talked about the importance of getting Supreme Court nominee David Souter confirmed.

It was a generic speech, but truth is, the vice president delivered it very well.

At the end, he thanked the crowd for the support it had given to Ashcroft, and he expressed his hope that the same support would be given to Milford.

Then, safely on the other side of the trucks, he landed.

Those of us who had come for a crash were left with only an empty feeling. The Mehlville High School band, under the direction of Don Kinnison, played "Columbia, the Gem of the Ocean," and the vice president left the podium.

Speaking of empty feelings, the band eventually was short-changed for lunch. The hotel didn't have enough hamburgers or Cokes.

But still, the kids got to play for the vice president, and that has to be a thrill.

Besides, if Evel Knievel ever makes a comeback and wants to perform to music, the kids from Mehlville ought to apply.

They can truthfully say that they've had experience with his kind of act.

Wednesday, September 12, 1990.

Circumstance, as much as talent, propels people into history, and so it is that Fred Williams has become the major player in what might be the most momentous event in St. Louis history.

Williams is the city's earthquake czar. He goes to work each day in his bunker-like complex under the Soldiers Memorial. From there, he directs the city's emergency management agency. That's the agency that will be in charge of things if we really do have the earthquake that some guy in New Mexico is predicting we might have.

If that awful event occurs, Williams will be The Man.

Not long ago, he gave me a tour of the bunker. Radios, maps, telephones. I t reminded me of a war room.

How strange it is to remember how it all started.

Williams was once an obscure state legislator. His one fling at notoriety occurred when he proposed a bill that would outlaw nose-blowing in restaurants, a practice he termed "disgusting."

His proposal was ridiculed. With all the problems facing the state — education, crime, a deteriorating industrial base — what kind of legislator worries about people blowing their noses in restaurants?

Williams didn't back down. Not the scorn of the press, not the pressure that surely came from the facial-tissue lobby, nothing deterred him.

In my favorite political speech, he defended his proposal. He said that normal nose-blowing didn't bother him. It was "honking" he objected to.

But his proposal went nowhere. Honking continued unabated and does to this day.

Shortly after his ill-fated efforts to stop the honking, he decided to run for mayor.

Insiders suggested that his decision came about only because Mayor Vincent Schoemehl, a political ally, was frustrated in his efforts to find a person named Freeman Bosley.

The real Freeman Bosley was running in the primary against Schoemehl. The most time-honored tactic in city politics is to dilute your opponent's strength by placing someone with your opponent's name on the same ballot.

Unfortunately for Schoemehl, the only other Freeman Bosley in town was his opponent's son, who wasn't about to undercut his father's support, especially since he already had a city job.

A couple of years earlier, Freeman Bosley Jr. had beaten Joe Roddy in the fight for Clerk of the Circuit Court, largely because young Bosley was able to find a woman named Clara Jo Roddy. This woman, who did not campaign and refused to be interviewed, split the Roddy vote, and on the strength of that split, Bosley won a very narrow victory. Had everybody who voted for a Roddy voted for the same Roddy, Bosley would have lost.

But hey, that's city politics. When a city election is really being contested, the ballot looks like a phone book.

At any rate, when Schoemehl was unable to find a Freeman Bosley to throw into the race, he resorted to another time-honored tactic. He decided to split the black vote.

In the city, there are, of course, two political parties — the black Democrats and the white Democrats.

Already the field was crowded with white Democrats. Former police chief Eugene Camp was running on the platform that the city owed him thousands of dollars in back overtime that the city was now refusing to pay. If elected, I will pay myself the money the city owes me, Camp vowed.

Alderman David Kinealy was running on the platform that an anonymous caller had urged him not to run.

Nobody tells me not to run! announced an angry Kinealy.

Only in St. Louis would somebody announce that he had decided to run because of a groundswell of people who didn't want him to run.

Although neither Camp nor Kinealy seemed like formidable opponents, the fact was the white vote was split, and Bosley was the lone black Democrat on the ballot.

Admittedly, some black Democrats had crossed racial lines to endorse Schoemehl. The most prominent, perhaps, was the head of the Aldermanic Black Caucus, Virvus Jones.

Nevertheless, Schoemehl knew that endorsements mean little. He needed to split the black vote.

Fred Williams filed.

Williams angrily denied reports that he had filed to split the black vote, but insiders suggested that Schoemehl was grateful.

Indeed. When Schoemehl won, he found a job in the administration for Williams.

Earthquake czar.

A fine job it seemed. The pay is good, more than $40,000 a year, and the duties seemed negligible.

Now all that has changed. The city readies for a possible quake.

Williams waits in his bunker, prepared to answer history's call.

Wednesday, September 26, 1990.

The Real Reasons Behind
The Latest Clinton "Affair"

Like most Americans, I love conspiracies. Consequently, I find this whole business about the Arkansas state troopers and their allegations about then-Gov. Bill Clinton's extra-marital affairs very interesting.

Why would they come forward with their stories now?

If the Republicans were behind it, the troopers would have been front and center during the campaign. Or else they'd wait until the next election.

As far as the Republicans are concerned, the timing here is awful. The president has plenty of time to rebound from this alleged scandal.

So I think we can eliminate the Republicans.

Truth is, only one person stands to gain from these latest revelations. That person is Hillary Clinton.

If I'm correct - and time will tell - we could be witnessing a historic coup.

The next step will be a dramatic one. Hillary will do what wives have always done to their cheating husbands. She'll kick Bill out of the house.

"I just need time to think," she'll tell him.

Bill Clinton will do what husbands caught straying have always done. He'll plead with his wife for a while, and then he'll find himself a small efficiency apartment.

The country will understand. After all, we all know couples who have had marital problems. The Clintons are just human, people will say.

In fact, I suspect most people will support Hillary. She's widely admired. She's smart, and she's tough. Besides, after the Gennifer Flowers scandal, she strongly hinted that she had had just about enough of being the good-hearted woman in love with a good-time loving man.

Remember when she said she wasn't Tammy Wynette?

So nobody will be too surprised if she gives him the boot.

It will seem odd at first, having a president trying to run the country out of an efficiency apartment. It will be unsettling the first few times we see photographs of foreign leaders sitting around the apartment complex pool while perfect strangers sun themselves on nearby lounge chairs.

But we'll get used to it.

Meanwhile, Hillary will continue to push ahead with her health-care reform. Political leaders will visit her at the White House to talk about the plan. Often, they'll discuss other issues of importance as well.

We'll start to think of Hillary as the real president.

And why not? She's certainly as smart as her husband. Smarter, probably. She's always been the bread-winner in the family.

Within a few months, Bill Clinton will be marginalized. Due to security reasons, the foreign leaders will no longer visit him at the apartment. Instead, they'll go the White House and talk to Hillary.

She'll finish her health-care reform and move on to some other big project.

Bill Clinton will pop up in the news again when the Los Angeles Times reports that he's dating a steward-ess who lives in the apartment complex.

"I have no comment," Hillary will say. "I'm trying to put together a welfare-reform package."

Suddenly, it will be 1996, and the Democrats will have to select their nominee.

Bill Clinton will call a press conference at the apartment-complex pool to announce that he intends to run for re-election. By the way, without his wife watching over him, he'll have fallen back into the habit of eating at fast-food establishments. He'll have put on a lot of weight.

Commentators will remark that it was a real mistake to hold the press conference at the pool. He looked like a whale in that bathing suit, Sam Donaldson will say.

The Los Angeles Times will report that the stewardess has dumped Bill. She and Bill will then discuss intimate details of their relationship on the Oprah Winfrey Show. During the show, Bill will come on to Oprah.

That very week, Hillary's welfare-reform program will be enacted by Congress.

Leaders of the Democratic Party will then urge Hillary to run against her husband. She accepts. She also files for divorce.

In January of 1997, Hillary Rodham is sworn in as the first woman president in our history.

The two Arkansas state troopers are given big federal jobs.

Could it happen? Sure. The country is ready for a woman president.

Will it happen? I think, fellow conspiracy buffs, that it has already started. There's no other explanation for what those state troopers are doing. Why go public now?

Only one person stands to benefit. Our next president.

Monday, December 27, 1993.

In Debate, Harmon Proved Himself a True St. Louisan

To a casual observer, it seemed that Clarence Harmon "lost" Wednesday's mayoral debate. That is, he didn't do as well as he could have. Perhaps Harmon was thrown off his game by some stinging personal attacks from gadfly candidate Bill Haas. Should he respond? Should he ignore? For the most part, he chose the latter course, but for whatever reason, he seemed somehow off-balance while Mayor Freeman Bosley Jr. plowed straight ahead.

In retrospect, though, I wonder if the subpar performance might not have been part of a grand design.

Maybe he wanted to look like a real St. Louisan.

In a recent profile in this newspaper, Harmon talked about a misperception he is constantly forced to address. People assume he's from somewhere else.

"They ask me things like, 'How long have you been here, and where'd you live before.' And I say, 'Beg pardon, I've lived here all my life.' "

Why do people assume he's an outsider? Probably because he seems too competent, too articulate.

Let's consider our history.

In this country's early days, when the civilization was based on and around the eastern seaboard, the successful people stayed put. They had no reason to leave. Only the less successful pushed westward.

Some of them ended up here.

This is a nice place, but it isn't the real west. The more adventurous of the less successful decided to keep going. This city became the jumping-off point, the Gateway to the West.

That is, of course, what the Gateway Arch commemorates. We are the only city in the world that built a monument to the people who left.

Sometime after a lot of mediocre white people established their roots here, the black migration from the south began. Most of these people were headed to Chicago. Others were headed to the auto plants of Detroit.

As in any great migration, you get a few people who drop out before reaching their destination. Hence, our city grew.

You can see the point I'm making. We were settled by unsuccessful people, and our population growth was fueled by the arrival of other unsuccessful people.

No wonder history passed us by.

That is not to say that this isn't a wonderful place to live. Especially if you're laid back. Sometimes I'm convinced that the Arch is a magnet for laid-back, unambitious people. It certainly drew me.

Even our home-grown industries reflect our nature. We are the center of the universe — Ground Zero! — for the brewing and motivational industries. Anheuser-Busch and Maritz Inc., the giants of their respective industries, are headquartered here.

That's us, all right. We like to drink beer, but we need to be motivated. Heck, the more we drink, the more we need to be motivated.

People with motivational genes left long ago.

No wonder Harmon has always seemed like an outsider.

I can remember talking to a friend about Harmon long ago. At the time, Harmon had just been named chief of police.

"I'd like to buy stock in that guy," said my friend. "He's going to be head of the FBI someday."

"Yeah, he's going places," I said. "I wonder where he's from?"

On the other hand, Freeman Bosley Jr. has always seemed like a St. Louisan. He's a decent guy, good company, fine fellow to have a beer with. Admittedly, things haven't gone so well on his watch. A scandal here or there, a company leaving here or there.

But really, that's business as usual. In case you've forgotten, things slid downhill during the last administration. Oh yeah, that last mayor, he was a real St. Louisan, too. Decent guy, good company, fine fellow to have a beer with.

Nevertheless — or maybe consequently — things slid downhill. But who got angry? Things have been sliding downhill since 1904. You see, despite our heritage, we were once a great city.

Quirk of geography. That's what it was. Right on the mother of rivers, smack in the middle of the country.

If some of the successful people who didn't come had come, or had some of the adventurous people who left had stayed, we would be bigger than Chicago.

Thank goodness it didn't work out that way. That's all I can say. Instead, we became a haven for underachievers, a home for the laid-back.

Because Harmon seems neither an underachiever nor laid back, he has always carried the aura of an outsider. In politics, that can be a real disadvantage. A candidate has to act like one of the people.

That's why I think Harmon may have underachieved in the debate on purpose.

If so, it worked. In the moments after the debate, a number of people told me they thought Bosley had "won." But nobody asked me if I knew where Harmon was from.

Friday, February 14, 1997.

Two Lucky Rich Guys: Dumb and Dumber

F inally we have conclusive proof that the rich are not smarter than the rest of us, just a whole lot luckier.

In fact, the real news here is not that the rich are not smarter than the rest of us — we've suspected that for years — but that they're dumber than we are. A lot dumber.

I'm talking about William Maritz and William Stiritz.

As you probably know, both of those fellows got extremely lucky this past summer. Shortly before Boatmen's Bank was bought by a larger bank from out of town, Maritz and Stiritz each bought thousands of shares of Boatmen's stock.

Stiritz bought 10,000 shares at $40.13 on June 21, and when the stock sank a tad, he bought another 1,300 shares. Three days later, he bought another 18,700 shares, also at $40.13.

The very day after Stiritz bought his final 18,700 shares, Boatmen's CEO, Andrew Craig, went to Atlanta for a meeting with the bankers who eventually bought Boatmen's.

When the sale was announced last month, the stock jumped to $55.50.

For Stiritz, then, we're talking about a paper profit of more than $450,000 from his June purchases.

Maritz had the same kind of good luck. In July, he bought 18,000 shares at $40.13. The next month, when the sale was announced, Maritz had a paper profit of more than $270,000 from his July purchase.

Normally, when a couple of already rich guys get richer in some quick stock deal, I figure, "Oh well, that's why they're rich. They're smarter than the rest of us."

But here's the interesting twist on this story. They aren't smarter. They didn't have a clue that Boatmen's was going to be sold, and that the stock would have that resultant big run-up.

You see, both Stiritz and Maritz are on the Boatmen's Board of Directors, and it would be illegal if they had made their purchases based on inside information.

It was all luck!

"There was no trading on any non-public information," CEO Craig told The Wall Street Journal. "Those transactions are clean."

I'm sure the St. Louis Man of the Year knows what he's talking about. If he says his directors were clueless, that's good enough for me.

But think for a minute about how dumb that makes Stiritz and Maritz.

After all, we have only two possibilities to consider. The first is that Craig went to Atlanta without telling his board.

That's possible, but hardly reasonable. In the past, when I've written critically about boards and have suggested that directors are grossly overpaid, businessmen have called to complain.

"Directors are more valuable than you think," one CEO told me. "When you're in charge, you need somebody to bounce ideas off of."

Selling the business is a pretty big idea. If you thought your directors were at all sharp, you'd certainly want to bounce that one off them. At the very least, you might mention that you were going to Atlanta to talk to the chairman of a big out-of-town bank.

Frankly, that should have rung a bell or two.

For months and months, there has been talk in the business community about local banks being takeover targets. Even I heard the talk. Surely, a couple of big-time guys — members of Boatmen's board, and presumably plugged into the banking world — heard the talk.

So fellows with normal intelligence might have figured something was up when Craig mentioned his trip.

But no. Our guys were obviously too dumb to put two and two together.

It was just a lucky coincidence that Stiritz bought 30,000 shares the week of the Atlanta trip. And when I say lucky, I mean lucky. Stiritz had been decidedly uninterested in the bank's stock until June. Despite being a member of the board, he had less than 3,000 shares before his big binge.

I am not being entirely sarcastic. There is reason to believe the "too dumb to figure it out" defense.

You see, both Maritz and Stiritz are extremely wealthy. The last time I checked Forbes magazine's list of wealthiest Americans, Maritz was on it. His fortune was estimated at $300 million.

Stiritz isn't quite in that category, but he's worth millions, too.

The Securities and Exchange Commission is serious about insider trading. At least, it pretends to be. Would these guys really risk going to jail just to pocket a few hundred thousand? They could probably find that kind of loose change in their sofas.

Any way you look at it, you have to conclude that neither guy is long on brains. And yet they're rich.

It has to be luck.

Friday, September 6, 1996.

Andy: Man of the Year

While we wait, along with the Itz Brothers — William Maritz and William Stiritz - to see how serious the SEC is about insider trading, let's consider another aspect of the recent sale of Boatmen's Bank.

The sale is just another reminder that it's time to retire the St. Louis Man of the Year award.

Our current champ, and hopefully our last, is Andrew Craig.

The award is given by rich guys to rich guys, and with a few exceptions, recent winners have been neither inspirational nor particularly civic-minded. Instead, they've just been rich.

For instance, there isn't much inspirational about Craig's story. Raised in a town founded by his great-great-great-grandfather, the young Craig became a banker.

Well, fine. Craig deserves some credit. It's possible for a young man to squander his advantages. It's also possible, of course, for a person to rise above the circumstances he or she was born into, but mostly, neither happens.

If you're of average intelligence and ability, you neither rise too high nor fall too far. Middle-class kids grow up into middle-class adults. Rich kids become rich adults. So if your great-great-great grandfather founded your hometown, and you become a successful banker, you're entitled to a pat on the back, but nobody is going to confuse you with Horatio Alger.

And civic-minded?

Craig just sold our biggest local bank to out-of-state interests. This is not good for the St. Louis area.

Of course, we shouldn't expect Craig to be thinking

about what's good for St. Louis. He's a banker, and a darned good one. He took a stodgy 148-year-old local bank and built it into a wonderful takeover target. Then he hired the New York investment firm of Goldman, Sachs & Co. and essentially auctioned our local bank to the highest bidder. He got a wonderful price.

He certainly will come out great. According to The Wall Street Journal, he stands to make $8.5 million in profit from his stock options alone. According to the St. Louis Business Journal, he negotiated a severance package that could give him another $3 million if he decides to bail out after a year. And he's 65 years old now.

That's all terrific. Nothing wrong with it. Nothing unethical about it.

Like I said, it's what we expect from bankers. They're bottom-line guys. Much of Craig's success, for instance, was the result of his takeovers — Centerre and Community Federal come to mind — and each of those takeovers resulted in massive layoffs.

"It's not easy, but that's my life," he once told a Post-Dispatch reporter when asked about the layoffs.

Sure it is. Again, though, that's the nature of the business, and the nature of the man. Craig is not Jimmy Stewart in "It's a Wonderful Life."

As regular readers might recall, I was critical when Craig was named St. Louis Man of the Year. A history of laying off St. Louisans hardly seems to be the credential we should be looking for, I remarked at the time of his selection.

Now, while still reigning as St. Louis Man of the Year, he's sold an important St. Louis institution to some guys from North Carolina.

He came out great. His shareholders came out great.

His pals, the Itz Brothers, came out great, at least for now.

But the region took a hit. Our biggest bank is now gone. The important decisions will no longer be made in St. Louis. They'll be made in North Carolina.

The impact of this is still unknown. So is the future of the people working in the soon-to-be defunct headquarters of the bank.

We do know, however, that this sale was not good news for St. Louis. A region never likes to see its big institutions owned by out-of-town interests. Remember how thrilled we were when the brewery sold the baseball team to local guys?

Maybe we should make August Busch III our St. Louis Man of the Year for not selling to out-of-town guys.

Forget that. Busch has probably already been Man of the Year.

That's another thing about the award. I'm afraid we're running out of rich guys. After all, we don't have a limitless supply.

After 41 years, the pickings get a little slim. You start running down the roster at the club to see who hasn't gotten it yet — yes, Craig is a member of the St. Louis Country Club — and pretty soon, you're down to the bankers.

Nothing wrong with bankers, of course, but as I've said, they're bottom-line guys. Given a choice between the city and the bottom line, they don't hesitate. And it's downright embarrassing when a St. Louis Man of the Year chooses the bottom line over the city.

Before we embarrass ourselves again, I say we retire the award.

Monday, September 9, 1996.

As I peer through the glass darkly at all things economic, it's comforting to know that I am not alone in my affliction.

In fact, there was a letter to the editor in this newspaper earlier this week in which the writer defended the Itz Brothers — William Stiritz and William Maritz — against those who would suggest the two had profited from insider trading. The talk of insider trading came about after the two directors of Boatmen's Bank made large purchases of the stock shortly before the stock zipped up on the news that the bank was being acquired by a larger bank from North Carolina.

Dismissing this talk as "sheer nonsense," the letter writer argued that a smart investor didn't need any inside information to know that the stock was a good buy. Discussing the price of the stock in August, the letter writer stated: "Now it doesn't take a genius to figure out that Boatmen's was a very underpriced stock even without the takeover rumors."

Not being much of a stock guy, I don't know. Maybe the letter writer has a point.

But don't tell it to Mary Wohlberg.

When her first husband died 15 years ago, he left her a trust, which was held, incidentally, at Boatmen's Trust Company, which is a subsidiary of Boatmen's Bank. A good portion of that trust was in Boatmen's stock.

On August 12, an investment officer from Boatmen's wrote Wohlberg a letter. He advised her to sell 900 shares of her stock.

"So far this year, Boatmen's has outperformed the market. I believe it would be beneficial to now take some profits in this holding, and to diversify into other securities," he wrote.

So she talked it over with her husband, and they figured that it was probably good advice. That's what I would have thought, too. I mean, a non-stock person might think it self-serving if the bank employee were to suggest buying the bank's stock, but if the bank employee thinks you should sell, you probably should.

She did.

Two weeks later, the deal was announced and the stock price jumped. Wohlberg lost about $13,000 by taking the bank's advice and selling the bank's stock.

Obviously, I am not the only one who doesn't understand economics — it could be the man who wrote the letter to the editor. After all, he made it sound like even a financial dolt could have seen, in August, that Boatmen's stock was a bargain and should have been purchased.

Chances are, he doesn't understand this stuff any more than I do.

On the other hand, what if the letter writer does understand? What if anybody with any sense could have seen that the thing to do was to buy, and not sell, the bank's stock?

That would certainly clear the Itz Brothers, who bought almost $2 million worth of the stock in June and July.

But what would it say about the bank?

If even a dolt could have seen that the stock was a buy, then the bank's trust department is being run by people who haven't even achieved dolthood. And they're giving financial advice to the bank's customers!

We've already been told that the Itz Brothers were clueless. That's fine. As long as you have a sharp CEO who doesn't need much advice — and apparently

Boatmen's Andrew Craig sought no advice before going to Atlanta to meet with the guys who eventually bought the bank — you don't need a lot of brain power on the board.

But if your trust department, as well as your board, is clueless, you're in bad shape.

How, then, can your stock be a bargain?

In defense of the trust officer, I should add that he wasn't alone in his recommendation to sell the stock. After the two directors loaded up on the stock in June and July, at least one other local broker advised his clients to sell. One client who took the advice wrote me a letter.

But people who know about these things defended the broker. It turns out that a lot of people looked at the insider buying as proof that the rumors about a takeover of Boatmen's were just that — rumors. That's because federal regulations bar directors of companies from trading on company stocks with the expectation of making a profit in a takeover.

In fact, the St. Louis Business Journal had a story about that shortly before the takeover was announced.

"Analysts said the purchases (by the directors) send a clear signal that Boatmen's is not likely to be acquired by another bank any time soon," the story said.

Just about the time that story was published, Mary Wohlberg sold her Boatmen's stock.

There is, of course, one happy footnote to this otherwise sad tale. Although she took the advice of the investment officer from Boatmen's, nobody is going to accuse her of profiting from inside information.

Quite the contrary.

Friday, September 20, 1996.

Free "Art" Advice: Get It While It's Hot

Memo to Hugh McColl of NationsBank:
This is our big week, partner. You're finally coming to town. You'll be here for Wednesday's annual meeting of the shareholders at the Adam's Mark Hotel.

If you slip away from the meeting and talk to a few average St. Louisans, I think you'll understand that I've been giving you some really straight scoop in these little notes that I occasionally jot out.

First of all, Hugh, you'll find that people don't like you. That is, they don't trust you. Part of the reason is that you're associated in the public mind with Andy Craig, and forget that Man of the Year stuff, Craig is very unpopular in this town. People are still upset that he sold our biggest bank to you, and a lot of people think it's just crazy that you guys have agreed to pay him $1.5 million a year for life after he retires. And his wife is going to get $1 million a year for life if she outlives him. All this on top of the $10 million in stock you gave him as part of the sale.

And in the meantime, you're cutting jobs and raising fees. It's crazy, Hugh.

Also, I've got to warn you about something. It might come up at the shareholders meeting. (I've been keeping my ear to the ground, just as I promised I would.)

Somebody might ask you about Kenneth Lewis. He's one of your North Carolina executives. He's probably pretty high on the chart, too. Last year, he had a salary of $750,000 and a bonus of $1.85 million.

People here don't know anything about this Lewis character, but a couple of weeks ago the Wall Street Journal had a big story about executive compensation and the way that some companies can cook the books and give the bosses even more than they say they're giving them.

The abuse the story cited was "moving expenses."

Based on what you've done with Craig, the people here figured that you're probably hip to this stuff — "Ain't no flies on Hugh when it comes to executive compensation" is the general feeling — so as soon as the shareholders got their proxy statements, they started looking for "moving expenses."

Sure enough, Lewis racked up a little more than $177,000 in moving expenses.

Where did you bring him from? Timbuktu?

Better expect some questions about that, Hugh. Forewarned is forearmed, eh? Speaking of questionable expenses, the proxy statement indicated that the bankpaid you $28,919 to have your taxes done. Who does them for you, your brother-in-law? I know accountants around here who'd do the job for $250 — as long as you're not trying any funny stuff, of course.

But your biggest problem still comes down to the art collection. You've got to use this shareholders' meeting to make an announcement that the Missouri art, which was collected long before Craig came on board, is going to stay here. It's got to go to the Art Museum.

I probably seem like a scold about this, and yes, I saw that I was quoted in your local newspaper, the Charlotte Observer, comparing you to the Visigoths who looted Rome.

Maybe that's overstating things, Hugh, and I apologize.

But I've been talking to reporters in your town, and

one of them — and I don't want to reveal my source here — told me you've got a new picture hanging in your office. Not surprisingly, the reporter doesn't know art from smart and couldn't tell me exactly what it was, but I got all worked up thinking you had one of those old Missouri pictures that the late Tom K. Smith went to so much trouble to acquire when he ran Boatmen's Bank so many years ago.

It was right after that that this other reporter called, and I was still hot; and that's when I called you a Visigoth.

On the good side, though, my little outburst assures that our friendship will remain on the q.t. Nobody will suspect that I'm sending you all of this inside information - to say nothing of the unsolicited advice. And I don't mean to be harsh about this, but you need some advice.

You're aware, I presume, that local institutions have already pulled about $2.2 billion from the trust department since the takeover. You've lost the Missouri Public School Retirement System, the Missouri State Employees Retirement System and the city cops' pension fund. Last week, the University of Missouri pulled $97 million from you.

This is not a good trend, Hugh. It can be reversed, I think, if you take advantage of your visit to our city and generate some positive coverage. Something about the art. Try it, Hugh.

Oh, and stay away from Andy Craig. You don't want to be photographed with him.

Monday, April 21, 1997.

If Not Jim, Who? If Not Then, Now?

I rise this morning in defense of a colleague, Jim Gallagher.

He's one of our financial writers. He is quiet, low-key and unassuming. He is methodical in his research, thorough and understated in his reporting.

Yet, he was subjected to a vicious verbal attack at the NationsBank shareholders' meeting Wednesday.

One of the shareholders drew a round of applause by criticizing an unnamed reporter for "salacious, unfair, incomplete, and inaccurate" coverage of the bank. This same shareholder apologized to NationsBank chief executive HughMcColl for the "slop" that has been written about him.

I made a quick check of our database to see who the shareholder was talking about.

It had to be Gallagher.

The only other person who has been writing about NationsBank and McColl is me.

As regular readers know, I have been offering advice to McColl. It's been good advice, sound advice, and offered with the most generous of intentions. Sadly, McColl hasn't taken much of it. Oh, sure, he announced Wednesday that the bank would not be selling the collection of Missouri art that it inadvertently acquired when it bought Boatmen's Bank. But my advice went beyond just not selling the art. Because the art was gathered long ago by Missourians for Missourians, I had suggested that McColl donate the art to the St. Louis Art Museum.

Not only did McColl reject that idea, he was downright insulting about it. He told the shareholders that he had no plans to donate the art to the museum but would, perhaps, consider it.

"We need to get to know some people better — to know it won't end up in someone's basement," he said.

That was, I thought, a real slap in the face at the people who run our Art Museum.

Can't Andy Craig vouch for the folks at the Art Museum? Admittedly, I don't think too highly of Craig, but McColl must. Not only has he guaranteed Craig a salary of at least $3 million for what seems like a make-believe job, he gave him $10 million in stock and is going to pay him $1.5 million a year for life after he retires. And if Craig's wife outlives him, she's going to get $1 million a year for life.

So he's got to like the guy.

Why can't he take Craig's word that the folks at the Art Museum know what they're doing?

But hey, this isn't about McColl or Craig. It's about Gallagher.

I've gone back and read his stuff. It's been measured and balanced. A little dry perhaps, but you've got to expect that when a guy is dealing with numbers. What's more, he has always been accurate.

In fact, I have used a lot of his research. I'd see him hunched over his desk, poring over various SEC reports and quarterly statements, looking like a character out of a Charles Dickens book.

"Hey, what we got, Jimbo?" I'd ask.

He'd wince at the Jimbo bit, but then he'd tell me what he had gathered, and I'd use the stuff, confident that if it came from Gallagher, I'd be all right.

And always it was.

Still, the shareholders cheered when his work was called slop. He stands accused of salacious and unfair reporting.

Those are strong words, and my initial reaction was to join the crowd, and perhaps earn applause myself by seconding the condemnation. After all, if you can't kick a man when he's down, when can you kick him?

But that wouldn't be right. It would be unfair. It might even be salacious, which, incidentally, I now suspect is a bad term. In the past, you could have said to me, "That was a salacious column," and I would have thanked you.

No longer. The shareholder who used the word to describe my colleague's work was not being complimentary. He was being mean.

What's to be mean about, is what I want to know.

Gallagher's numbers seem to show that the shareholders are doing fine. McColl will do as he pleases with the art. Andy Craig, our former Man of the Year, is doing especially well.

When a reporter — maybe it was Gallagher — asked about the millions of dollars Craig is getting out of the whole affair, Craig shrugged it off.

"These numbers are large, but this is a very large company," he said.

Indeed, it is. Still, workers get laid off, banking fees go up and Craig gets $1.5 million a year for life after he retires, and his wife gets $1 million a year for life if she survives him?

To me, that's salacious.

I don't think Gallagher has done such a bad job.

Friday, April 25, 1997.

M ore than a week has passed and Allan Cohen, the general manager of KMOV-TV, Channel 4, has not heard from a lawyer, so apparently there won't be a lawsuit.

That's good news for the station, which certainly would have lost. As any attorney will tell you, jurors tend to sympathize with an average citizen who suffers because of something a big company did. The potential for suffering was indeed great recently when Channel 4 made a grievous mistake.

The station incorrectly identified the winning lottery numbers.

Actually, what the station did was mix up the Illinois and Missouri lotteries. The winning numbers for Illinois were run as the winning numbers for Missouri, and vice versa.

A few minutes after the mistake, the station corrected itself.

But, hey, by then it was too late.

Imagine you've turned on the news to get the latest lottery results. The anchorperson reads the numbers as they're flashed onto the screen. You've got your tickets in front of you.

You've got the first number, then the second, then the third, then the fourth, then the fifth, and then — can it be? — you've got the sixth!

BINGO!

You think you'd stick around to watch the rest of the news?

Of course not. By the time the anchorperson corrected the error, you'd be dancing in the street.

You're free!

There's the joke about the guy who's sitting in a bar when he sees the results on television.

First thing he does is call home.

"Hey, I just won the lottery! Pack your bags!"

"Terrific, honey. Should I pack summer things or winter things?"

"I don't care. Just be out of there by the time I get home."

Even those of us who wouldn't leave our spouses would almost certainly leave our jobs. After all, in this time of high unemployment, it would be immoral to hold a job when you don't need to.

A lot of working people have even rehearsed the speech they'd deliver to the boss if, and when, the Good Ship Lottery lands.

Most of these speeches — at least most of the ones I've heard people practice — are very unflattering to the bosses.

I mean, this isn't Japan. Workers and bosses don't get along.

So when I heard the television people make their mistake, I imagined some poor Joe thinking his life was about to change. Which would be true, but not in the way Joe imagined.

First, he'd call home and tell his wife to get packing. Then he'd buy the bar a few rounds.

He'd probably celebrate all the way to Monday morning, at which time he'd stumble into work.

Oh, the fun he would have!

Into the office he comes, still wearing the clothes he wore Friday night, looking unshaven and dirty. Wait, scratch that. When you're poor and dirty, you're dirty. When you're rich and dirty, you're eccentric.

His pals would stare at him as he marches toward the boss's office. A quick wink at his pals, and then into the lion's den.

He'd give the speech he'd been rehearsing all weekend.

Yes, he'd tell the boss what he really thought.

"I'm not sure what I'm going to do with my millions, but you'd better hope I don't buy the company," he'd say, or something to that effect. Most of the speeches I've heard include a line like that.

Finally, he'd go to the lottery office to turn in his winning ticket.

He'd learn the truth.

So he'd have to call his wife and say, "Look, honey, I was just kidding about winning the lottery, and I was kidding when I said those things about younger women. The truth is, I love you, and I need you. Especially now, with me out of work and all."

The next morning, after a fitful night of sleep on the couch, he'd have to go back to the office. His wife would demand that he at least try to get his job back.

Oh, the humiliation of his return!

Back he comes, retracing his steps from the day before.

"You gonna tell him off again, Joe?"

This time, though, there's no wink for his pals, no glide to his stride. This time, he shuffles toward the boss's office.

"Those things I said about you, that's not really the way I feel," he stammers.

But, hey, the speech was a bridge-burner. It's out the door.

Back to the saloon.

With luck, though, there'd be a lawyer at the saloon. He'd overhear Joe talking to the bartender.

Had that happened, Joe would be more than rich. He'd also be the owner of a television station.

Monday, March 20, 1989.

Reserved Veteran Flushes
Clinton from the Pocket

I t is entertaining, if sad at the same time, to watch the dream of a new NFL franchise seemingly slip away.

Maybe entertaining isn't the right word. Maybe instructive is the word we're looking for.

You see, this is a quintessential St. Louis story.

Let's think back to when we were supposed to be a lock for one of the two new franchises. Our "team" consisted of James Orthwein, Jerry Clinton, Fran Murray, and Walter Payton.

The two main players were the two St. Louisans, Orthwein and Clinton. Orthwein had the cash, and Clinton had the plan.

In St. Louis, which has a caste system only slightly less rigid than that of old India, they were an odd couple. Orthwein was Old Money, and Clinton was New Money.

The two were almost cartoon characters.

James Busch Orthwein. Connoisseurs will tell you that the middle name is the best way for Old Money to reveal itself.

That's because Old Money is understated, and dignified, and avoids the limelight.

Although Orthwein is the second-largest stockholder of Anheuser-Busch, most of us common folk had never heard him of him until he joined the St. Louis NFL Partnership in the summer of 1990.

Shortly after Orthwein joined the Partnership, a sportswriter from this newspaper asked him about his relative anonymity.

"I don't know of anybody that a lot of publicity has helped in this world," said Orthwein.

New Money is loud, and brash, and loves to be on center stage. That pretty much describes Clinton.

You want a quick, unscientific study of the two men?

In the three years before the Partnership was founded, this newspaper published 14 stories in which Orthwein's name was mentioned.

Almost half of those were "society" or horse-show stories. No quotes. The bulk of the remaining stories were about a suit involving a brokerage firm. In only one of these stories was Orthwein directly quoted. In two others, he issued a brief statement.

Meanwhile, in the same time period, Clinton's name was mentioned 64 times. These stories ranged from politics to sports to charities to business. He was quoted in many of these stories.

In some cities, especially cities that are growing rapidly, New Money and Old Money mix easily. Not here. This is the city, you might remember, where Edward Whitacre, the bossman of Southwestern Bell, couldn't gain membership in the "right" country clubs.

For the Clinton-Orthwein alliance to last, Clinton had to make certain adjustments. That is, he had to tone himself down. He had to act — how shall we say this? — more respectable.

But Clinton suffers the fault of so many self-made men. He's so darned proud of where he came from, and how far he's come, that he assumes that everybody else is as impressed as he is with his success story.

So he wears his hardscrabble background like a medal. He talks about growing up in a housing project. He calls himself a street-fighter.

Old Money is not impressed.

Quite the contrary. Old Money is put off. Clinton is not the sort of guy Old Money wants to be partners with.

Sadly, a breakup was inevitable.

And when Orthwein left — technically, he's still an investor — he took his checkbook with him.

That left Clinton with Murray, a former hot-dog salesman with a checkered financial past, and Payton, a former football player. Neither fellow has any St. Louis ties. More to the point, neither has the kind of money you need to buy a franchise.

Consequently, St. Louis turned to John Connelly, a businessman from Pittsburgh.

Whenever we turn to Connelly, it's a sign of desperation. After all, he regularly plays Professor Harold Hill to our River City. The first time he came calling, he told us we had trouble with a capital T, and that rhymed with B, and that stood for Boat.

So he bought the Admiral, and then sold it back to us for a fat profit, and then he got it back again, and now that riverboat gambling has been approved, he stands to make an even bigger killing.

Happily, Connelly is a fellow who makes no distinction between Old Money and New Money. He likes All Money.

Ah, but there is always a rub. While Old Money may have been willing to bankroll the new franchise and then take a back seat while New Money ran the team, Smart Money is not about to trust somebody else to manage his investment.

So this deal never really had much chance, and the dream of a new franchise continues to slip away.

Oh, well. We should have seen it coming when Orthwein and Clinton first hooked up. In St. Louis, Old Money and New Money just don't mix.

Wednesday, September 29, 1993.

Kroenke May Find Life in
Limelight Is Somewhat Sour

The very first telephone call I received Tuesday morning came from a concerned citizen who wanted to know if I had seen the front-page photograph of E. Stanley Kroenke.

Yes, I did see it, I said.

Everybody here at the plant is talking about it, the caller said. We've all agreed that the guy is wearing a cheap toupee.

Let me look into it, I said.

Then I leaned back, and wondered if Kroenke had any idea what he might be getting himself into.

He is, by all accounts, a private person. Very, very rich, but very, very private.

He mentioned his penchant for privacy to the assemblage of reporters, photographers, commentators and other sub-professionals who gathered at a press conference Monday afternoon. The press conference had been called so our civic leaders could introduce Kroenke as the Daddy Warbucks who was willing to adopt our orphaned effort to get an expansion team.

Having spent the morning at Jerry Clinton's press conference, I was aware, of course, that the reason our effort was orphaned was that our civic leaders had just finished shooting the original father.

Oh, well. Our civic fathers taketh away, and they giveth.

Right after Kroenke explained that he was a person who valued his privacy, he asked for questions.

"What's your net worth?" asked one of my colleagues.

Geez, I wish I'd asked that, I thought.

Kroenke, who seemed to think, mistakenly, that the reporter was joking, laughed uneasily. Actually, everything he did he did uneasily. He stood at the podium uneasily. He talked uneasily. He responded to questions uneasily.

"Refreshingly undynamic," I jotted down in my notebook. "Charmingly befuddled."

Then I thought about an interview I had years ago in Arizona with an artist named Ted DeGrazia.

DeGrazia was a colorful character who had achieved fame and fortune late in life. There were many years, he told me, when he couldn't trade a painting for a bottle of whiskey. Now, those same paintings are worth thousands of dollars, he said.

How has success changed you? I asked him. He was wearing old clothes. He looked like he hadn't shaved in a week.

"Success hasn't changed me a bit," he said. "What it has done is change the way people think of me. In the old days, I was a drunk. Now, I drink just as much, but instead of being a drunk, I'm an eccentric."

I thought about DeGrazia on Monday afternoon, and I looked back at my notes. I scratched out "Refreshingly." I scratched out "Charmingly."

Ah, that's better, I thought. Undynamic. Befuddled. That's an accurate description of the way Kroenke seemed Monday.

The rest of the fellows seated at the long table with Kroenke had the air of easy confidence that great wealth or great power confers. With the rest of them, the description "self-assured" comes to mind. Sometimes, the appropriate word is "arrogant."

But never "befuddled."

Of course, let's be fair about this. People who know Kroenke say he has always avoided the limelight. They say he's smart, but quiet. So, of course, he was uncomfortable Monday.

Let's forget fairness, and be downright charitable. Maybe the reason Kroenke seemed so befuddled had to do with something Andrew Craig, chairman of Civic

Progress and the emcee of the press conference, said when he described the new partnership. He said, "The group is made up of people who are substantial."

That happens to be one of my favorite words. It's so much more descriptive than "rich."

Because — let's face it — anybody can be rich. I could buy a lottery ticket with my next six-pack, and, if I was incredibly lucky, I could become rich. But I wouldn't be substantial.

And one thing substantial people absolutely hate is when a large group of unsubstantial people shout questions at them. Especially when one of the questions is, "What's your net worth?"

After laughing uneasily for a moment, Kroenke realized he was supposed to answer the question.

"Well, that's certainly a personal question," he said. He hesitated, uneasily, of course. "I appreciate the question," he said.

But he didn't. Sometimes substantial people say the opposite of what they mean!

All this is meant to suggest that the perfect team owner would be a rich guy, but not a substantial guy. It's a measure of our desperation that we were forced to turn to a substantial guy.

In a way, then, maybe Kroenke got a reprieve when the NFL announced only one team Tuesday night. Maybe he'll eventually be able to return to a substantial anonymity.

Oh, as far as the toupee question goes, I did look into it. I talked to an attorney from Columbia, where Kroenke is from.

"That's his own hair. Absolutely," said the attorney.

I'm sure Kroenke appreciates our interest.

Wednesday, October 27, 1993.

Sadly, Some of Us Just Don't Have the Right Jeans

Thanks to the reaction of an outraged public, Levi Strauss & Co. has agreed to continue supplying jeans — at least through the end of the year — to Donald Rathert's country store in Red Bud, Ill.

Normally, when the public succeeds in imposing its will on a company, the public rejoices. In this instance, though, the public mood remains troubled.

There is much soul-searching going on.

It can be traced, I'm afraid, to one of the comments made by Julia Hansen, Levi's manager of retail and distribution initiatives. One of the reasons she had cited in the company's original decision to cut off Rathert's supplies was that his store — a humble country store — did not mesh with the company's customers.

Levi Strauss customers, she said, had a self-image of "sexy, rebellious, secure and successful."

In other words, Madonna.

Well, fine. There's nothing wrong with a jeans company having a target audience of Madonna. She is probably a wonderful person. Her book, as I recall, sold very well. She must be a talented writer.

But still, Hansen's remarks left the rest of feeling unfulfilled, especially those of us over 30.

There was a time, you see, when most of us aspired to sexy, rebellious, secure, and successful. Then age and time and gravity dampened our ambitions. Truth is, most of us would now settle for any one of the four.

Maybe not rebellious. At least not alone. If it came in a package deal with successful, that would be terrific.

At any rate, here we were, the public, forced to take a long hard look at ourselves to determine if we are even entitled to wear Levi's.

Are we sexy?

Sure we are! Well, sort of. OK, maybe not very. Depends on whether we're dealing with people with good eyesight.

Rebellious?

Hardly. Most of us are just trying to get along.

Secure?

In this era of downsizing, only an idiot would feel secure. Besides, the older you get, the more you realize that a jillion things could go wrong any minute. We're all crossing a big lake on some very thin ice.

Successful?

That depends, I suppose, on how you define it. If you want to define it in traditional terms — that is, financial terms — forget about it. Most of us are living paycheck to paycheck. In fact, I was talking to a fellow who works at a car dealership. His job is looking at people's credit and getting people authorized for car loans, and he told me it's just mind-boggling how little money most people have. Sad to say, my mind wasn't boggled.

In the past, I have written about life's great disappointments. I remember, for instance, writing about President's Day. That's the day in every young man's life when he realizes he will never be president. It comes shortly before Senator's Day, and is followed, sometimes quickly and sometimes years later, by Boss's Day.

But still, we persevere.

This Levi Strauss thing has been difficult, however. To realize we are flawed and imperfect and not destined for greatness is one thing. To realize we do not meet even the standards for buying blue jeans, well, that is another thing entirely.

One reader who shares this angst sent me a copy of a letter he sent to the president of Levi Strauss & Co.

"I'm sure you and your expensive marketing people know your business better than I, but I have reservations about the niche market you seem to be going after," wrote Wilbur Rittenhouse. "Of the 100 or so people I saw on the street this morning (OK, it was only 11:30 and the rebellious were probably not out in force yet), I would rate only two as sexy, and they seemed neither secure nor rebellious. One may have been wearing Levi's, but though I walked pretty fast for a fat, old guy, I couldn't get close enough to be sure. (Be cool, I was not wearing your stuff.)"

Who would have thought it would come to this, that out of courtesy, we would feel compelled to assure the blue jeans company that we don't wear their stuff?

The only good news, I guess, is that there are so many of us who are unqualified to wear the company's jeans.

Even if you dropped the requirement of sexy as being too nebulous — the old roadhouse definition stipulates that people become more sexually attractive as closing hour nears, and Ms. Hansen did not say if the company's customers were 9 o'clock sexy or 12:55 sexy — we still have a problem with the co-mingling of rebellious and successful. Few of us are both.

It would be a tragedy for Levi's to disappear from the American scene. I hope Madonna buys a lot of them.

Friday, January 24, 1997.

Of All the Gin Joints,
She had to Pick This One ...

C hicago - I was sitting at the bar in a little joint on Wabash Avenue right under the elevated tracks. Now and then, a train would thunder past and the television screen at the end of the bar would go fuzzy. Didn't matter to me. The president was giving his acceptance speech, and had I wanted to hear it, I could have used my press credentials to get into the convention hall.

Instead, I had come to this joint. It's a place from out of my past.

I was on my third whiskey and water — I've done too much drinking this week — when I heard the voice behind me.

"Hello, Sailor."

I had known that if she wanted to find me, this was the place she'd come. We used to have lunch here that summer we met so many years ago. I had been working at a small haberdashery on State Street when she came in to buy something for her father.

"Aren't you going to ask me to sit down?" she said.

"Sure. Sit down, Hillary," I said.

She was wearing a wig and dark glasses, but truth is, she didn't need much of a disguise in this establishment. Most of the clientele wouldn't have even recognized her husband.

"I thought you were at the hall," I said. "In fact, a couple of minutes ago, I saw you on television."

"Computer-enhanced hologram," she said. "Don't tell me you're not hip to that. You're not one of those people who think we really landed a man on the moon, are you? You've got a lot of faults, but naivete didn't used to be one of them."

She ordered a club soda with a dash of lime. I asked

the bartender to touch up my drink. He splashed some more whiskey into my glass.

Hillary gave me a disapproving look. I ignored it. "Oh, come on," I said. "There're worse things than having a drink. Just ask your friend Dick Morris."

"He's a Republican," she hissed.

I almost pointed out that she was a Goldwater Girl when I knew her, but I stopped myself.

"He might be a Republican, but he's acting like a Democrat," I said.

It's true, too. In the old days, before party lines got blurred, you generally needed an accountant to catch a Republican. With the Democrats, an eye at the key-hole was generally enough. They were a lustier group.

"You're in a nice mood," she said sarcastically. "I thought you'd be happy to see me."

I apologized. This has been a difficult week for me. Fun, but difficult. Mostly, there have been the memories of what might have been. Democratic conventions in Chicago can do that to me.

I'm talking about what could have happened in 1864. The Democrats had a convention in Chicago that year, too. They nominated the great George McClellan. History buffs will tell you he lost the general election to Abe Lincoln, the Republican incumbent.

Had there only been television in those days, the results would have been different. George was a handsome fellow. Thick eyebrows that grew together, long sideburns, a full mustache. The camera would have loved him.

But there was no television, and George got crushed. The family never recovered. It was, we like to say, our high-water mark, and we've been on the skids ever since.

Now it has come to this. In the very town where my ancestor got the party's nomination, I can't even get an invitation to the best parties.

I guess I shouldn't be surprised. Jimmy Carter didn't even get an invitation to the convention until it was embarrassingly late. He ended up skipping the whole thing. Short memories these Democrats have.

Speaking of good parties, Hillary had one Wednesday afternoon at the Billy Goat Tavern on lower Michigan Avenue. That's a newspaper hangout, and I've been spending a good deal of time there. But when Hillary had her party, they chased out the regulars to let the swells in.

Back when George Bush was president, he had lunch at the Billy Goat and the regulars were allowed in. Now the Democrats are chasing the regulars out. Back in 1864, the Democrats were the party of the people.

"I read about your party at the Billy Goat," I said pointedly.

"Ernie Banks was there," she said. "So was Sara Paretsky."

Paretsky, of course, is the author who writes the V.I. Warshawksi private eye books. "Oh yeah, Paretsky," I said. "If you were inviting authors, you might have thought about me."

"Seriously? You wrote a book?"

"True crime," I said. "Paperback. Came out a couple of years ago."

She shrugged dismissively, as if to say she doesn't read true crime books. I told her I hadn't read her book, either.

Having exhausted our literary conversation, we turned toward the television. Her husband was saying something to the effect that our best days are still in front of us. A train thundered past, and his words were drowned out and his image flickered.

"So what do you think our chances are in November?" she asked me.

"You guys will win going away," I said. "This Morris thing won't change anything. Your husband is a great talker, and he'll demolish Dole in the debates."

She smiled.

"I've got a question for you, Hillary. Back in St. Louis, we're pondering the future of Dick Gephardt. But all the so-called informed sources say your husband's going to throw his full support to Al Gore. What's the truth?"

She hesitated for a moment.

"Maybe the country will be ready for the first woman president," she said.

"You mean you?" I asked.

She shrugged. On the television, the realistic-looking hologram was applauding.

Friday, August 30, 1996.

IV

Life Is Just a Peck

I t looked as if the Reverend E.H. Truman was going to be upstaged for sure.

How embarrassing, I thought. The Rev. Truman is the pastor of the Leonard Missionary Baptist Church at 1220 North Grand. A funeral was being held in the church and the Rev. Truman was officiating. He was scheduled to deliver the eulogy.

But the deceased had a lot of relatives, and some of the relatives had requested that the pastors of their churches be allowed to speak at the funeral.

The Rev. Truman had graciously consented.

So two ministers and a deacon each got a chance to address the congregation.

And let me tell you, those fellows could speak!

One of them, it was the deacon, I think, talked about the songs the congregation sings every Sunday. Songs about going to heaven. Songs about laying down life's burdens. Songs about living in the light of the Lord forever.

"You sing these words every week," he reminded his listeners. "And I'm saying to you that Brother Howard (the deceased) is living those words right now. He has laid down life's heavy burdens."

Well, I'm a white man in a white man's society, so I don't carry some of the burdens that the rest of the congregation has to carry, but still, the deacon's words seemed to lift a load off even my shoulders.

And, clearly, the words struck home to the rest of the congregation. No way around it, the deacon could talk.

One of the other ministers then got up, and right away you could see that he had an inside track. He was related by marriage to the deceased.

So he talked in a kind of family-to-family style, real

personal is what it was, and the rest of us felt privileged just to listen. It was almost like being able to sit around a kitchen table and hear the wisest man in a family impart a dose of wisdom to the rest of the family during a family crisis.

He ignored the rest of us as he gently lectured the family about the significance of death. I don't remember exactly what he said, but it was about loss and triumph and inevitability. He was good, as good as the deacon, and that's saying something, believe me.

The other minister was no slouch, either. He talked about death being nothing more than birth. His was a message of joy.

The music, by the way, was terrific. The Inspirational Choir sang a song with a chorus that went something like, "I'm so glad Jesus said to me, everlasting life is free." That had a special significance because utilities, unlike everlasting life, aren't free, and the deceased had frozen to death after Laclede Gas Co. shut off his gas.

When the three speakers had finished, and the music was done — the Leonard's Male Chorus also did a number — it was time for the Rev. Truman to deliver the eulogy. I felt sorry for the man. No way could he top the previous speakers. At least, that's what I thought.

But he did. He walked slowly to the podium, and he nodded at the pianist, who began playing what sounded like a soft blues song. And the Rev. Truman started talking about being a young boy, and playing in a cemetery. He said he noticed something on all the tombstones, and even as a boy, it had seemed strange.

"There were always two dates," the Rev. Truman said. "The date of birth, and the date of death. And in between those dates, brothers and sisters," and then he paused, "there was just a dash." Then the Rev. Truman asked the congregation how many of them ever used a typewriter. It's interesting, he said, how you make a dash on a typewriter.

"It's just a peck," he said. "A dash is just a peck." Then he paused again, said something to the piano player, and turned back to the congregation. "Life is. . . just a peck," the Rev. E.H. Truman said, and one of his parishioners, digging on the profundity of it all, punctuated the pastor's statement with an "Amen."

It's been two weeks now since the Rev. Truman delivered that eulogy, and I can't get it off my mind. And the more I think about it, the more I think he's right. And if he isn't right, what the heck. I'll still pass it on.

Life, brothers and sisters, is just a peck.

Wednesday, January 11, 1984.

Man's Smile Masks Life's Lost Promise

Shortly after 4 a.m., the alarm clock rings.

"Play ball, play ball," says Jim Stoien.

He cleans up, and walks through the cluttered living room of his one-bedroom apartment. He walks with a limp and a slightly sideways gait. His right arm hangs uselessly at his side. He goes into the small kitchen and makes himself a breakfast of pancakes.

After breakfast, he grips the handle of the shopping cart that he stores just inside the door. With his good arm, he pushes the cart out and heads toward Jewish Hospital four blocks away. It is now 6 a.m., and the city is stirring to life.

At the entrance to the hospital, he picks up a stack of 100 newspapers that the carrier has left for him. He takes the elevator to the top floor, and goes door to door, selling the newspapers and dispensing good cheer.

"Play ball, play ball," he says to people.

He finishes his rounds on the top floor, and works his way down, floor to floor, room to room. He's been doing this for years — he started in 1981 — and he has earned almost complete access. Pushing his cart loaded with newspapers, he winds his way down the halls.

He has the same deal at Barnes Hospital, which is where he goes after he finishes his rounds at Jewish.

He makes 13 cents per paper.

He is a familiar and cheerful figure at the two hospitals, this seemingly retarded man with a sideways gait and a limited vocabulary.

"Hi, Jim."

"Play ball, play ball."

In addition to the Post-Dispatch, he delivers the various free newspapers that get dropped off at the hospital complex. These, of course, he delivers for free.

189

He delivers them because it's what he does. He delivers newspapers.

He used to do other things. He can't remember what they were. But he knows about these things because he has photographs and papers.

One of the papers is titled, "Post-Irradiation Effects of Photoreactivating Light and Caffeine on Cultured Marsupial Cells Exposed to Ultraviolet Light."

He presented that paper at a seminar in April 1975. He was, at the time, a 28-year-old National Science Foundation scholar working on a doctoral degree in microbiology at the University of Colorado.

"Years ago, years ago," he says with a shake of his head.

Before becoming a doctoral student, he was a lieutenant in the army. He served in Germany. He has photographs and papers to prove it. Before the army, he was a student at the University of Missouri. He has a student identification card to verify it. And before that, he graduated from McCluer High School. He has his yearbook from 1964, the year he graduated.

He must have been popular. He was one of 10 young men selected for homecoming court. He's smiling out from page 201. An attractive young girl is holding his arm.

Before moving to Florissant in time for high school, he was a city kid. He grew up with his mother, three brothers and three sisters in the Cochran housing project.

"He was the man of the family," his mother says.

"Jim was always the star," says a younger brother. "He was the only one of us who got a college degree."

Not only a bachelor's degree, but a master's. A commission in the Army. And then, almost a doctorate.

In October 1975, he was riding his bike home from campus when he was struck by a car. He was in a coma for eight weeks. When he regained consciousness, he was transferred to the Veterans Administration Medical Center in St. Louis.

"The patient does not speak or groan," the admitting physician wrote. "He does not follow commands but looks about the room in all directions."

Several months later, still unable to speak, Stoien was discharged. The prognosis was not good.

Four and a half years after his accident, Stoien spoke. According to medical papers written about his recovery, the onset of speech was sudden, dramatic and completely unexpected. He counted to 10. He said his name. He said he wanted a beer. He laughed and laughed.

It has now been 14 years and one week since he stunned the doctors with his dramatic recovery. His speech is still halting, and he's more comfortable with a few well-worn phrases — "Play ball, play ball" and "Years ago, years ago," and "Gotta get a girl" — than with sentences and casual conversation.

But his halting speech is not indicative of his intelligence. He lives alone, cooks his own meals, and washes his clothes. He balances his checkbook. He takes the bus to Busch Stadium for baseball games. According to his family, he never forgets a birthday.

Of course, he is not what he once was, and he knows it. He reads, but with difficulty. He remembers nothing about life before the accident.

"Years ago, years ago," he says.

Sunday, April 17, 1994.

Life and Death on the Streets

T ulio Tim told Paul Acsay, his former parole officer, about his plan to move to Florida.

Acsay was reminded of Ratso Rizzo from "Midnight Cowboy." It's strange, but when Acsay told his wife about his conversation with Tulio, that association is what came to her mind, too. "She said he'd never make it. She said he'd end up like Ratso, dying on the bus," Acsay says.

A lot of people who knew about Tulio's plan thought it was doomed to failure. On the other hand, nobody could be sure. Because Tulio Tim Ninteman, a totally unsocialized 27-year-old child of the St. Louis streets, had something going for him that Ratso Rizzo could only dream of.

That's money.

Tulio Tim was going to receive about $20,000 from an aunt's estate, according to officials from the city's public administrator's office. The aunt died in December of 1980, but certain legal problems — not the least of which was that Tulio Tim had no address — kept things balled up. Officials say Tim probably would have received the money sometime this summer.

Whether the inheritance would have allowed Tulio to succeed where Ratso failed, whether he would have been able to reach that place "where the sun keeps shining, through the pouring rain" is a matter of some doubt.

In fact, it's a matter of a whole lot of doubt.

"Tim couldn't handle that kind of money," says Acsay. "He would have got drunk and lost it or gotten rolled or maybe he'd have given it away. Money was something he didn't understand."

There were a lot of things Tulio Tim didn't understand.

Women, for one.

"I don't think he ever thought about sex," says Sherry Browning. "He had no concept of things like family or women or love. I mean, he knew in a vague way that those things existed, but they didn't have any relevance to him."

Mrs. Browning, who works as a counselor for Goodwill Industries, was the woman in Tulio Tim's life.

In his death, too. When he died this month, the cops called Mrs. Browning. They didn't know who else to notify. In one of Tulio's pockets, the cops found a crumpled piece of paper on which was scrawled Mrs. Browning's name and number.

"The first thing I thought was that he froze to death," says Mrs. Browning.

It was nothing that dramatic. The medical examiner's office has not yet determined the cause of his death, but it was, if you're willing to stretch a term, a "natural death."

Glue-sniffers aren't known for longevity, and although Tim was off the stuff by the time he died, the toluene he had inhaled as a kid — it was his penchant for toluene that earned him the nickname Tulio Tim — had already taken its toll. Tim was also an alcoholic and an epileptic who generally refused to take his medication. He ate irregularly and he slept in vacant buildings and parks.

"I used to tell him he was 27 going on death," says Acsay. "But Tim, he thought of himself as a survivor."

Whatever romantic notions you might have concerning street characters — and Tulio Tim was the best-known street person in St. Louis — there was nothing glamorous about Tulio's life. He was, in a word, a loser. He had been arrested more than 70 times, usually for petty offenses — drunk and disorderly conduct, trespassing, begging, general peace disturbance. His most celebrated arrest occurred on the riverfront during last summer's Veiled Prophet Fair. In the midst of a million drinkers, Tulio Tim managed to get pinched for drinking in public.

There had been other, more serious charges. The most serious involved a fight behind the Sunshine Mission on Christmas Day of 1979. Tulio knocked a guy's eye out. He did 15 months for that.

But if Tulio Tim did little with his life except self-destruct, he accomplished something with his death. The members of his family finally met one another.

It happened at his funeral.

Mrs. Browning, who had tried so hard and so often to help Tulio Tim, showed up with her husband. John Silvernail, a cop who has seven children of his own but still found time to befriend Tulio Tim, showed up. Silvernail even paid for the flowers. Acsay and several colleagues from the state's parole and probation department showed up. A couple of people from the New Life Evangelistic Center, which had sheltered Tulio Tim from more than one storm, were there.

Tulio Tim's family.

The whole thing reminded Acsay of a conversation he had had with a co-worker a couple of months earlier.

Tulio had come into the office, more or less to check in with Acsay, but also to say hello to some of the other parole officers. That was pretty standard. During last year's snowstorm, Acsay ordered Tulio to come by and at least knock on the window by Acsay's office every day, just so Acsay would know Tulio had survived the night.

At any rate, when Tulio left the probation and parole office on the day in question a couple of months ago, Acsay's co-worker wondered aloud when Tulio Tim's parole would be up.

"Oh, it's up already," Acsay said.

"Then why does he bother to check in every day?" the co-worker asked.

"For the same reason you go home every night, " Acsay said. "I guess he just wants to see his family."

Monday, February 21, 1983.

Policeman's Death Disturbs the Peace

F rank Graham came to this country from Scotland, and he was energetic if not ambitious.

He joined the Marine Corps and fought in Korea. He got married and eventually had five children. He was a mechanic for McDonnell Douglas Corp. He made good money. But something was missing. He didn't want to be a mechanic. He was a people-oriented guy. He decided he wanted to be a cop.

Frank was two years too old to become a cop. He was 37. But if you took away the years he spent in the Marine Corps, he qualified. Those years were taken into consideration, and Frank became a University City policeman.

He also was active in the community. That's an understatement. He was the leading light behind the University City Athletic Association.

It would be unfair to say that Frank loved any of his children more than the others. But his oldest daughter, Monica, was always called "little Frank." That was partly because she looked the most like Frank. She also imitated her dad. He whistled all the time. Monica whistled all the time.

He was also her coach. He coached her softball team from the time she was in third grade to her freshman year in high school.

Frank somehow found the time to go back to college. He was seeking a degree in criminal justice. He wrote a paper about a day in the life of a patrolman. He wrote about writing tickets. He wrote about burglaries. He wrote about answering a family disturbance call.

Those are the worst kind of calls for a cop. Everybody is angry. The disturbance call Frank wrote about was pretty typical. In the beginning, the wife demanded that Frank arrest her husband. In the end, the wife declined to prosecute. Frank convinced the husband to leave.

"Peace is restored," Frank wrote. "Or is it?"

For Frank, peace meant family life. Every Sunday, he took the family somewhere. Usually, it had something to do with sports. On Feb. 22, 1976, which was 10 years ago last Saturday, Frank took his family to Forest Park. They spent the early afternoon sledding on Art Hill.

Then Frank took his family home, and he went to work.

That night, there was a call on a family disturbance. Frank and his partner, Joe Didden, answered the call. It seemed routine.

While Frank and Joe tried to calm things down and make sense of the situation, the husband left the room. He came back with a shotgun.

Monica was only 14, but she knew the truth when she saw the sergeant at the front door.

He didn't have to say anything.

It took Monica a long time to come to grips with the situation. Her dad was dead. I've seen the papers she wrote in high school, and those papers are about the loss she felt.

Her dad would be proud of her. She finished high school and went to Fontbonne College. She got school loans. She now teaches at the Central Institute for the Deaf. She's doing well, and she says the rest of her family is doing well, too.

I visited her Saturday night, on the 10th anniversay of her father's death.

"He was such a remarkable person," she said. "He was so giving."

We talked about her dad for quite a while. She laughed about the fact that she was called "little Frank." She's 24 years old now, and she said she still whistles, but she can't recall any of the songs her dad used to whistle.

"They were songs from Scotland," she said.

She had nice things to say about her mother.

"After all, Dad took a pay cut to become a policeman, but Mom never complained. Maybe that says something about Dad," she said.

Monica's husband came into the room while we were talking. He never knew her father, but he knew of him.

"I played hockey in University City, and everybody who was involved in sports knew of him," Monica's husband said.

Monica's husband, whose name is Bob Fanning, met Monica through sports. Bob used to play hockey with Monica's older brother. Bob met Monica at her brother's wedding.

Bob and Monica got along great right from the start. There were some shaky moments, though, when Bob told Monica what he intended to do with his life.

He said he wanted to be a cop.

"She sort of rolled her eyes," Bob said.

But that got straightened out, and Bob became a cop in University City in October 1981. Bob and Monica got married in June 1983.

The three of us laughed about the turn of events on Saturday night. Then Bob had to go to work.

I left a little before Bob had to, so Monica and her husband could say their goodbyes in private, on the 10th anniversary of Frank Graham's death.

Friday, February 28, 1986.

In Unsettled Times, God Builds House on Higher Ground

Austin Deery used to dream of a house. It would be big, if not splendid. He went so far as to make a down payment on a piece of land in Jefferson County.

At the time he made this investment, he was living in a trailer with his wife and six children. Being a carpenter, Austin had built an additional room that was attached to the trailer, but still, it was crowded. What's more, his wife, Sherry, was pregnant again.

He needed a house.

Not that Austin didn't know a thing or two about crowded conditions. He was the youngest of eight boys and the 12th of 16 children born to Patrick and Mary Deery of the small town of Buncrana in County Donegal, Ireland.

They were working-class people.

Seven years ago, at the age of 27, Austin left Ireland and came to this country. He settled in St. Louis and met Sherry. She was divorced and had three young children.

He was smitten with her children and they with him.

"The boys were 5 and 6, and I remember one of them asked Austin on that first night, 'Would you like to be our father?' I was embarrassed, but I think Austin was charmed," Sherry said.

Sherry and Austin were married in the fall of 1990. They soon had three more children, and a fourth on the way.

In the fall of last year, Austin made his down payment on a small piece of land. Months earlier, he had quit his job with Agape Construction, and had formed his own carpentry and construction company. It had not yet turned the financial corner, but Austin was confident. He was convinced that everything would work out.

He was killed last October in a one-car accident. He had no savings, and no life insurance.

I visited Sherry and her children last week.

They are living in a new four-bedroom house. It is not on the lot that Austin was buying. That lot was on low ground. The new lot is in the same subdivision, but it is on a hill.

Outside the house is a sign: This is the House that God Built.

Immediately after Austin's death, friends from the evangelical Christian community — Sherry is a member of the Christian Life Center — rallied around the family. Chief among these friends was Kevin O'Brien, a member of the Kirkwood Road Christian Church and the owner of Agape Construction.

"I guess I was the Nehemiah," he told me, referring to the Hebrew leader who rallied his people to rebuild the walls around Jerusalem.

While donations from friends in the Christian community poured in, O'Brien told associates in the construction business what he intended to do.

Everybody chipped in. The owner of the property volunteered to switch Austin's lot to the hilltop lot. A man cleared the trees for free. An excavator dug the foundation lot for free. The foundation was poured, and the only cost was for materials.

In the meantime, I had written a story about Austin's death and O'Brien's intentions — that's all they were at the time — and the list of volunteers and donors swelled.

Electricians and painters and plumbers and heating and

cooling people — most of whom knew O'Brien from work — either worked for free or gave large discounts.

The owners of a lighting fixture company — Austin had done carpentry on their home — called and told Sherry to pick out whatever fixtures she needed.

A stranger in the brick business called and offered to supply however many bricks were needed. The bricks eventually went into the fireplace.

Sherry and the children moved into their new house in late September. Without a mortgage, Sherry and the kids are able to get by on the Social Security they receive because of Austin's death. What's more, her church established a trust fund, and Sherry figures that if she's careful and frugal, she may not have to return to work until at least most of her kids are in school.

The baby, born four months after his father died, is 10 months old. The other preschoolers are 3 and 4.

On the night I visited, Sherry had just put the Christmas stockings on the mantel. There were nine stockings, one for each of the kids, one for Sherry and one for Austin.

"I feel like he's here," Sherry said. "It's a miracle."

O'Brien is characteristically modest about what he has accomplished.

"My prayer is that God gets the glory," he told me.

Incidentally, during the months of work, O'Brien made sure that each day's labor began with a prayer, and it was the same prayer every day.

"Let there be peace in this house."

As the carpenter's family prepares to spend its first Christmas in their new home, one thing is certain. There is indeed peace in the house that God built.

Sunday, December 22, 1996.

Priest Helped Rich, Elderly
Parishioner — And His Reward Is Great

The two elderly sisters — Ada and Estelle Nolan — lived alone in a large house on Clement Street in the small town of De Soto.

Neither had ever been married. In the spring of 1983, Ada was hospitalized with terminal cancer, and it was clear to everybody that she would never be coming home.

But Estelle was not alone in this very difficult time. Her parish priest, the Rev. John H. Schneider, was there to help.

If the church had recruiting posters, Father Schneider would be on them. He is tall and handsome. He is very well-spoken. Charismatic is a word that often comes up when people are asked to describe the priest who became Estelle's special friend.

Estelle, a devout Catholic, lived frugally, but she was a very wealthy woman. The public adminstrator of Jefferson County estimates that her estate is worth, even now, between $750,000 and $1 million.

Father Schneider volunteered to help his elderly parishioner with her finances.

It was, as Father Schneider said last month in a deposition, "a friend helping a friend."

One of the first things the friends did was establish a living trust for Estelle. An amendment to that trust named Father Schneider the "successor trustee" to succeed Estelle upon her death or incapacity.

The advantage of a trust, opposed to a will, is that with a trust the property passes directly to the beneficiaries without having to go through probate proceedings. The documents Estelle signed awarded the bulk of her estate to Father Schneider.

To further clarify matters, Estelle signed a new will

to comply with the terms of the newly established trust. Father Schneider was named executor of this new will.

"Basically, she wanted me to have everything," Father Schneider said Friday, in an interview at the rectory of St. Martin of Tours parish in south St. Louis County, where he now is associate pastor.

But, Father Schneider said, he told Estelle that he didn't want to end up in a fight with her relatives.

"I asked her to give them something. So she gave $10,000 to each of her four nieces and one nephew, and $10,000 to the church," he explained.

The rest was to go to the priest.

The friends also established a joint checking account at a bank in Hillsboro. The monthly statements, and the canceled checks, were sent directly to Father Schneider.

From May of 1983 to April of 1984, Father Schneider wrote checks worth a total of $135,631.14.

One of the checks was for $31,000.

In a deposition, Father Schneider said that check was used to pay off his parents' mortgage.

"It's something she really wanted to do," he said Friday.

Another check was for $38,000.

That check, according to court records, went to PaineWebber. In a deposition, Father Schneider said $25,000 of the money was used for an annuity, and the remainder went toward a zero coupon bond. Incidentally, when Father Schneider established the account at PaineWebber, it was not a joint account. It was in his name only.

Most of the rest of the $135,000 is hard to trace.

In a deposition, Father Schneider says that some of

it went for a down payment on one of the two $18,000 cars he bought while he was helping his elderly parishioner with her finances. Some of the rest of the money went for trips and vacations, he said in a deposition.

But court records and Father Schneider's depositions indicate that at least some of his trips — most notably, a trip to Brazil and a trip to Santo Domingo— were financed with credit cards, which were paid through a different account of Estelle's.

According to his deposition, Father Schneider would visit Estelle every Wednesday for lunch, and at that time, he would pay her bills, using her second account.

"If I had an expense, I would say, you know, here is mine, and she would sign the checks," the priest said in a deposition.

Bills he presented for payment included his credit card bills, his federal tax bills, his car payments, his alumni dues from Kenrick Seminary and even bills from Capsulized Communications Limited.

"That was stories and thoughts for preaching on Sunday," he said in a deposition.

According to papers filed by the public administrator of Jefferson County, Father Schneider spent more than $200,000 of Estelle Nolan's money.

In our interview Friday, I asked Father Schneider if he had ever worried about the propriety of spending so much of a parishioner's money.

"It isn't like I sat down and wrote a check for $135,000," he said. "It didn't seem like that much. I was staggered when they counted it."

Father Schneider's annual salary is $8,000.

"I never felt that I was taking advantage of her,"

Father Schneider told me. "She was very generous with me."

I asked Father Schneider, who is now 47 years old, how he would describe his relationship with Estelle, who is now 89 years old.

He talked about how isolated and lonely she was when Ada died.

"Her life had been devoted to her family. She never married because she had taken care of her mother. So when Ada died, and there was no one around, she was reaching out to me," he said.

Estelle's former housekeeper, Louise Hayes, said she believed Father Schneider wanted to keep Estelle lonely and isolated.

"I wasn't supposed to take her anywhere," she said. She had been hired, incidentally, by Father Schneider.

She also remembered a more playful relationship than the one Father Schneider recalled.

"He'd make me leave whenever he came over. When I came back and he got ready to leave, he'd always say something like, 'Take care of my beautiful girlfriend,'" Hayes said.

Whatever the relationship, it ended in February of 1986. Estelle revoked the trust.

The priest responded by filing suit claiming that Estelle was mentally incapacitated and should not be able to revoke the trust.

"I just wanted to find out what was going on," Father Schneider said Friday.

Estelle gave a deposition in May of that year. She called Father Schneider "a dirty rascal." She said, "I never had anything to hurt me so badly in all my life."

In September of 1986, Estelle's estate filed a counterclaim against the priest.

Late last year, Estelle became ill. In February of this year, she was declared incompetent, and Samuel Rauls, the county public administrator, was appointed her guardian and conservator *ad litem*. He filed suit against the priest. Rauls contended that the priest had taken family heirlooms, jewelry, a coin collection and furniture, in addition to the money.

Earlier this month, the case was settled out of court.

Estelle's relatives and Rauls, acting on behalf of Estelle, agreed to drop all claims against the priest. In return, he agreed to assign the PaineWebber account to Estelle. He also agreed to return a coin collection.

The agreement also specified that no party to the agreement was accepting "culpability."

As long as nobody is accepting culpability, far be it from me to assign any. But maybe there is a lesson to be learned.

In one of his depositions, when he was trying to explain why he took $38,000 of an elderly parishioner's money to open an account at PaineWebber, Father Schneider remarked that "the archdiocese does not have a retirement program."

For the sake of its parishioners, if not its priests, the archdiocese ought to establish one.

Sunday, October 22, 1989.

"Miss Mattie Passes," but Her Spirit and Soul Food Live On

F irst came one telephone call. Then a second. Then a third. Each of the callers used the same words.

"Miss Mattie passed."

It seemed absolutely appropriate that such an old-fashioned term — an echo from a different time — was used to describe the death of Mattie Myers, who was born 79 years and 10 months ago.

Regular readers know that Miss Mattie presided over Mattie's Dinette, the most successful soul-food restaurant in St. Louis.

She was born in Mississippi, and she came to this city as a child. She graduated from Sumner High School and then went to beauty college. She opened the Smart Set Beauty Salon, but she was more an entrepreneur than a beautician. Before long, she owned a couple of cabs. Then she opened a bar.

She was always successful because she worked so darned hard, but none of those businesses were exactly what she was looking for.

And then, 40-some years ago, she opened a restaurant. It was as if Van Gogh had been trying to write novels and suddenly discovered painting.

In addition to working 12 hours a day six days a week, Miss Mattie had a simple philosophy.

"I give them good food, and lots of it," she told me several years ago, when I first wrote about Mattie's Dinette.

Another reason Miss Mattie was so successful was she followed her own precepts, many of which are written on plaques and hung on the walls of the dinette.

One of those precepts is this: "Let no one do more for you than you do for them."

Because Miss Mattie considered that first story a kindness, and because she followed her own rules so faithfully, she sent me $50.

I called a mutual friend. I can't take this money, I said.

Then donate it to the Annie Malone Home for Children, the friend said. It's one of Miss Mattie's favorite charities.

Miss Mattie must have sensed my discomfort. Although I continued to periodically write about Mattie's Dinette, she never again sent me cash. Instead, she fed me.

I thought about that when the Rev. Herman Gore Jr. was delivering the eulogy at Miss Mattie's funeral Monday afternoon.

"She fed a lot of people for nothing," he said. "The homeless, the poor."

I felt guilty, until the preacher continued.

"She fed me so much for nothing that I had to quit going," he said.

Maybe he had to quit going for moral reasons. Or maybe he was talking about the fact that the food was so good you couldn't help but overeat. Either way, I knew what he was talking about.

In fact, if I didn't come from such an uptight heritage, I would have said, "Amen, Brother."

Happily, many of the people in the overflow crowd weren't so uptight, and when the Rev. Gore said that actions always speak louder than words, and that Miss Mattie wrote her own sermon every day just by living the way she did, a lot of the people voiced their assent.

"She wrote her own text! Every day!" he said.

In addition to kindness, hard work was a fundamental part of that text.

"Success is a matter of luck. The harder you work, the luckier you get," reads one of the plaques on the walls of the dinette.

Oh, did Miss Mattie practice that one. I remember a birthday party she threw for herself several years ago during which she spent a good deal of time in the kitchen helping prepare the dinner.

Thinking about that, I missed the next part of the eulogy, but I brought myself back as the Rev. Gore was talking about the rapture, and admonishing the audience that we would need reservations to catch that flight, but none of us should worry about Miss Mattie because she had her ticket.

The service ended on that uplifting note. The only unsettling feature of the program was the non-appearance of Edith Bland. She has been an employee of the dinette for more than 25 years, and the program notes had said that she would be speaking.

She didn't show up.

Tuesday morning, I stopped by the dinette to visit. I spoke with Bertha Pointer, the chief cook and the person who has been managing the dinette during these last few months while Miss Mattie has been ill.

Where was Edith yesterday? I asked.

Bertha looked pained.

"She felt bad about not going. You know Miss Mattie was more than a boss to us. Maybe it had something to do with the fact that she never had children. We were her family. That's why she always did us like she did."

Sure, but where was Edith yesterday?

"She was cooking," said Bertha.

I nodded. So Edith missed the funeral to prepare for the dinner rush.

Miss Mattie has passed, but at the dinette that bears her name, her successors are still reading from the text that she wrote every day of her life.

Wednesday, December 22, 1993.

Kilby's Roots Don't Mean He Curries Favor

J ust last month, state Rep. Craig Kilby told the world that his uncle had been homeless for 20 years.

Kilby, a Republican from Lake Saint Louis, revealed this painful family secret after a number of do-gooders criticized him for his seemingly callous attitude toward the less fortunate. Perhaps you remember the furor.

Voters in St. Louis County will be asked in the November election to approve a $3 increase in the fee for filing a document with the recorder of deeds.

The money would be used for emergency shelters and programs to prevent foreclosures on homes.

Some officials in St. Charles County thought the proposal should be extended to their county. At least, let the voters decide, the officials said.

Kilby spoke out strongly against the idea.

He said that homelessness was not an issue in his neighborhood.

"People in my district know how to take care of themselves and their families," he said.

He meant, of course, that most Republicans know how to inherit money.

Presumably, Kilby knows how to do it. His biography in the state manual proudly points out that he's a 10th-generation American.

Of course, this makes the revelation about his homeless uncle all the more poignant. Why didn't the uncle — who was, after all, a ninth-generation American — learn how to inherit money?

At any rate, the people who run the various social-service agencies declared that Kilby was heartless. In response to this criticism, Kilby trotted out the story about his homeless uncle to prove that he did, indeed, care about the homeless.

His problem with the proposal to help the homeless had to do with priorities, that's all.

"I've got other legislation I want to pursue that affects a greater number of people," he explained.

Like other concerned citizens, I waited eagerly to see what this legislation might be.

Earlier this week, Kilby unveiled his plan.

Flanked by several stable owners, Kilby held a press conference and announced his intention to sponsor a bill that would make it difficult for foreigners to sink their teeth into Missouri horses.

Such legislation has become necessary, Kilby says, because a French company plans to open a horse-slaughtering plant in St. Francois County.

Which is true. To the surprise of most of us, who thought the French ate only frog legs and snails, it turns out that horse meat is considered something of a delicacy.

Oh, those crafty Frenchmen!

For years, we've thought they were a cultured people. When reruns of "The Lone Ranger" were such a hit in France, many of us thought they liked the music.

"Those Frenchies will watch anything if it starts with the 'William Tell Overture,' " we said to ourselves.

But no. They weren't interested in the music. They weren't interested in the story lines. They were staring at Silver, wondering what kind of wine would go best with the trusty steed.

Red with a bay, white with a palomino.

Kilby really hit the roof when he learned what the French company intended to do to Missouri horses.

Being a 10th-generation American, he has a special affinity for horses.

His own ancestors used to ride horses to court when it was time for them to inherit their money.

Besides, horses are pets, Kilby declared.

"People invest a lot of feeling and emotion in these horses, and you don't want them just hauled off for hamburger."

Of course, you don't.

As things stand now, a lot of Missouri horses are shipped to slaughterhouses in Texas or Minnesota, where they are turned into dog food.

Under this system, these horses are consumed, for the most part, by American dogs.

Surely, that appeals to a 10th-generation American like Kilby.

Of course, there will be detractors. As this battle heats up, you can be sure that somebody will point out that Kilby does not represent St. Francois County. These detractors will argue that the people of that county ought to decide if they want the jobs that the French company will provide.

On the other hand, if the working people of St. Francois County have not learned how to inherit money, too bad for them.

What's needed here is a compromise, something that wouldn't offend Kilby's sensitivities but would allow the people of St. Francois County to secure employment.

Maybe the French company should be allowed to slaughter only homeless horses.

There are more of them than you might imagine. Even Silver might have had a homeless uncle.

Friday, September 21, 1990.

A Life of Courage, a Message of Love

erri and David met at a softball game. She was a waitress. He was in sales.

They dated, and then they got married. That was 10 years ago. David was 30. Terri was 28.

The only sad thing about the marriage was the fact that Terri could not get pregnant. So Terri and David decided to adopt. They talked to three agencies and picked up papers from each, but before they sent the papers back, Terri got pregnant.

Cody Armstrong was born in July of 1988.

He was born with pneumonia. Shortly after his birth, the doctors told David and Terri that their newborn son would probably die within two days. David and Terri were devastated.

"It went from being the happiest day of our lives to the saddest," David said.

But Cody surprised the doctors. He survived the first day, and the second, and then he began to get stronger. He spent the first two weeks of his life in the hospital, and then he went home. He was perfectly healthy.

When Cody was 2, David and Terri had another child. Shaylyn Armstrong was born in January of 1991.

Cody loved the role of Big Brother. When Shaylyn would cry, Cody would go over and pat her head. He was always gentle with her.

Otherwise, he was a typical little boy, a rough and tumble kid. Before his third birthday, he was playing tee-ball.

He didn't stay with tee-ball long. Instead, he wanted his father to pitch to him. Day after day in the back yard, David would pitch and Cody would hit.

So it went in the spring and summer of 1992.

One evening in early September, David came home ready to pitch — and Cody said no. He had a headache. He was tired.

David and Terri figured he had a cold.

After Cody continued to feel lethargic for several days — it was so unlike him — David and Terri took him to the doctor.

He's got a sinus problem, the doctor said. Because Cody also seemed dehydrated, the doctor suggested he spend the night in the hospital. After a night hooked up to IVs, Cody felt much better.

But David and Terri were persistent about the headaches. Were the doctors sure there was nothing wrong with Cody?

The hospital did a CAT scan.

David was at work when the results came back, and he drove to the hospital to pick up his wife and son. Cody, who felt so much better, came running down the hall to meet him, but Terri looked stricken.

"Brain tumor," she whispered to her husband. He almost passed out.

Later that month, the doctors operated to remove the tumor.

"I don't want you to get your hopes up," the surgeon told David and Terri. "It looked malignant."

Tests indicated that the surgeon had been right. The tumor was malignant. It was a form of tumor rarely found in children.

But David and Terri never gave up hope. Neither did Cody. The surgery had left him partly paralyzed on his right side. As winter turned into the spring of 1993, he began to regain his strength. Although he still had very limited use of his right arm, he wore a

Velcro glove on his right hand so he could still swing his toy bat.

During that winter and early spring, he had seven magnetic resonance imaging tests done on the tumor. The news was good. The tumor seemed inactive.

The eighth test was conducted in April. The tumor was growing.

This time, his parents were prepared. They had been reading medical literature and talking to doctors all over the country. They took their son to Duke University. They were looking for a miracle.

After four days of treatment, the doctors said it was hopeless.

David and Terri and Cody returned to St. Louis.

Cody seemed strong and healthy until June 18, which was David's birthday.

Then his condition worsened. For three days in late June, he seemed to slip in and out of consciousness. On June 27, David and Terri called a visiting nurse to come to their home. He looks bad, they said.

"He's in a coma," she said.

David carried his son into the living room. He sat down in a recliner, and held his boy in his arms. It felt good. For the past few days, Cody had been in pain and uncomfortable and had not wanted to be held.

"It's OK to die, Cody," David told his son. Terri said the same thing. Both had read that children will hold on to life because they don't want to disappoint their parents.

"When you get to heaven," said Terri, "paint me a rainbow in the sky. Then I'll know you're all right."

Cody quit breathing.

The next night, Terri's parents came over for dinner. It was a stormy afternoon. Lightning and thunder cracked in the dark sky. But after dinner, the rain seemed to slacken, and David walked to the window.

A huge rainbow stretched from one horizon to another.

So spectacular was this rainbow that it was the lead item on the 10 o'clock news. One station interviewed an 80-year-old man who said he had never seen such a beautiful rainbow.

You can be sure that in the Armstrong house, the story of Cody's rainbow will be remembered this Easter Sunday.

Incidentally, Terri and David are expecting another child in August. This child will never know Cody, but like the rest of the family, he or she will be reminded of him whenever a rainbow paints the sky.

Sunday, April 3, 1994.

Twilight Turn:
Nun Loses Home among Sisters

Margarite Cookson, who was born on Valentine's Day in 1917, lives in a nursing home in Jefferson County. Her roommate died not long ago, and so for at least the time being, she has a small double room to herself. Mostly, she stays there. In her wheelchair, in her room.

She is not accustomed to living with strangers. Especially male strangers.

Margarite is a nun.

In the order of the School Sisters of Notre Dame, Margarite Cookson is known as Sister Mary.

For many years, she was a teacher. Now she is something of a pioneer. She was in the first wave of nuns to be sent to secular nursing homes.

That happened in March, and it represented a dramatic shift from past practices.

In the past, elderly and infirm nuns spent their last days at church facilities. The School Sisters of Notre Dame, for instance, went to Villa Gesuin north St. Louis County.

They lived there with other sisters and the comforting routine of the religious life. A daily Mass was offered.

To an outsider, it must have seemed timeless.

Gradually, though, the world was changing. The population of sisters was growing increasingly older. Fewer young women were joining.

Eventually, caring for the elderly sisters presented a philosophical problem — education, not nursing, is the mission of the order — and when that problem was addressed by hiring laypeople to provide the care, another problem loomed.

Money.

Villa Gesu is not a licensed nursing care facility. It is, instead, a religious home. Although Medicare will pay for medical procedures, Medicaid will not cover the cost of long-term care.

It will kick in, however, if the nuns are in secular nursing homes.

"We started looking at this problem a couple of years ago," said Sister Kathleen Koenen, provincial councilor, a member of the leadership team for the order. "We had to do something."

The decision was made to phase out Villa Gesu. Although there are still approximately 100 elderly sisters there, the order intends to transfer them to nursing homes and sell the facility within two to four years.

Sister Mary Cookson was in the first group to leave Villa Gesu. She was one of seven nuns sent to Corey Manor in Jefferson County shortly before Easter. Her roommate, a 99-year-old nun, died two days after the move.

"We were told it was a financial burden," Sister Mary told me when I visited her last week. "We resented it a little."

For the most part, though, Sister Mary seemed cheerful enough and much preferred to talk about the old days. She shook her head vigorously when I asked if she felt betrayed or if she had any second thoughts about giving her life to the church.

"Not at all," she said.

In 1931, she entered Rosati-Kain High School, which was staffed by the School Sisters of Notre Dame. Margarite was impressed with the sisters, enchanted with them, and when she graduated in 1935, she became a novice and moved into the Motherhouse just off Broadway in St. Louis.

There were, she said, 48 young women in her class. These days, the order gets a new sister about every other year.

In 1937, Margarite became a sister. She taught at an elementary school on Market Street for 10 years, and then she was sent to St. Clair, where she served as a principal. Then she went to a school in Robertson.

As a teaching sister, she did not receive a salary. Instead, the parish would give the money to the order, which, in turn, provided Sister Mary with whatever she needed. Always, she lived simply.

In the late '60s and early '70s, she worked with alcoholics at St. Louis State Hospital. Then she went back to teaching. Somewhere along the line, she earned a degree in English from Fontbonne College.

As recently as three years ago, she worked as a tutor for young people who were brought to the Motherhouse for instruction.

About two years ago, she moved to Villa Gesu. In an unspoken way, it was a retirement. The last stop.

Then in March, she was moved to the nursing home.

"We asked who would be willing to go, and she said she was willing. It wasn't like she volunteered, but she was willing," said Sister Kathleen.

The sisters at the nursing home conduct prayer services three times a week, and once a month, the local parish sends a priest over to conduct a Mass, and really, Sister Mary could do with more regular services, but she's not complaining. She said her friends from the Motherhouse often come by for visits.

Besides, she has her memories of a full life, given wholeheartedly to the church.

Sunday, May 25, 1997.

Raise a Glass to Dying Breed

The name of the story on the AP wire was "Barosaurus," and I was disappointed to see that it was about a scientific controversy.

It turns out that the National Museum of History in New York has displayed a statue of a barosaurus, which is a type of dinosaur, rearing up on its hind legs. This pose is credible, according to the article, only if you believe that dinosaurs are related to the birds of today. Apparently, this is a very hot subject among scientists. There are even those who believe that dinosaurs had feathers.

That sounds like an interesting notion, but still, I was disappointed.

I thought the article was going to be about men.

In case you haven't noticed, men are currently the rage of the publishing world. Not men per se, but the men's movement.

According to these authors, the men's movement is helping us discover our "true" identity and come to grips with our "true" problems.

The way we worked out our problems in the old days — with a couple of drinks — is out of fashion.

So I thought "Barosaurus" was going to be a story about how men who hang out in bars are becoming extinct.

"He was a barosaurus when she married him, but he's a wimposaurus now."

That sort of thing.

It's true, of course. Men have changed.

I blame Lamaze.

In the old days, men had almost nothing to do with babies. Except for passing out cigars, we had nothing to do with the act of birth.

"If men had babies, there wouldn't be any controversy about abortion," a feminist friend once told me.

"If men had babies, there wouldn't be any people," I replied.

But now, thanks to Lamaze, fathers are present at their children's births, urging the mothers-to-be to breathe.

As if they wouldn't, otherwise.

That kind of fifth-wheel involvement continues as the children grow up.

We don't do nearly as much as mothers do, and we expect to be complimented all the time for the little that we do — "Hey, I folded the laundry! Aren't you going to say something?" — but still, we do more than our fathers did.

It's difficult to be a barosaurus if you're helping out at home.

Maybe Lamaze should share the blame — or the credit — with the economy. A lot of women are in the work force today.

They work all day, come home and cook dinner, and they're not so tolerant of a man who arrives late for dinner all the time.

A barosaurus is always late for dinner.

It used to be quite common for a man to stop at a saloon and have a couple of quick ones after work.

In fact, the barroom crowd was almost like a second family, and the bartender was like a big brother or big sister. Somebody you could confide in.

Oh yes, when I think back on those days, they have a Garden of Eden quality to them.

The barosaurus was a happy animal. I see him now — drinking, laughing, smoking.

But then, unfortunately, driving.

Society has become very aware of the drunken-driving problem. And thank goodness for that. But still, in our righteous zeal to get drunks off the road, we snared many a barosaurus.

Slowly, then, their numbers dwindled.

The country's obsession with fitness hurt, too. A barosaurus is seldom slim.

The crusade against smoking hurt, too. When a barosaurus quits smoking, it's hard to hang around the gang at the old watering hole. Too much temptation.

And what about the neo-prohibitionists who argue with ever increasing fervor that alcohol is a dangerous drug? With a wary eye on this movement, the breweries run ads about moderation.

In retrospect, one can see that almost every change in the country's social fabric in the last 20 years has had a negative effect on the amiable barosaurus.

Conspiracy buffs could argue that somebody — a woman? — long ago devised a plan to destroy the barosaurus.

Maybe there's truth in that.

Ironically, as the barosaurus was being driven toward extinction, Hollywood decided to capitalize on the plight of the poor beast. So television gave us "Cheers."

Ah, Norm! Ah, Cliff!

When I saw the story slugged "Barosaurus," I thought somebody had finally addressed the whole subject.

Instead, it was a story about dinosaurs. Maybe they had feathers.

How irrelevant the story seemed. Dinosaurs are long gone. The barosaurus still exists, but its days seem to be numbered.

If you know one, buy him a drink. Someday, you can tell your grandchildren.

Friday, January 17, 1992.

A Bad Break? To Him, It's Just One More

Grant Hartman stopped by with a story the other day.

His clothes were clean, but hardly fashionable. Like me, Hartman is a fellow who puts on a shirt and pair of pants in the morning and leaves them on for the rest of the day. What's good enough for work is good enough, period. Because Hartman works as a custodian, what's good enough for work is never anything special. I met him several years ago when I worked as night police reporter.

For more than 23 years, Hartman worked as a custodian at the police station. He always worked the night shift, and he specialized in cleaning restrooms.

The pressroom has a small restroom, so every night — while I sat around with Rich Kurre, my friend and competitor from the Globe-Democrat, waiting for the citizens to commit mayhem on each other — Hartman would come in with his scrub brush, his bucket, and the other tools of his trade.

He talks very slowly. He walks unsteadily, as if he's been drinking, but in fact he does not drink at all.

Scarlet fever is to blame.

Hartman contracted the disease 64 years ago, about the time of his first birthday.

Appearances to the contrary, the fever left his mind intact, although, as he says, he does everything slowly.

Sometimes on quiet nights, we talked. Hartman was very much resigned to the fact that scarlet fever had robbed him of a normal life. He has no wife, no children. He lives in a rented room at the Salvation Army's Railton Residence.

One night he was robbed on his way to work. He did not seem overly excited about it, and, I later learned, he had been robbed before. Once, he was badly beaten by the robbers.

Well, sure. If you live and work downtown, and you work the night shift, and you walk to work because you don't have a car, and you walk funny, as if you've been drinking, you're going to occasionally be a victim.

It's something you accept, just as a suburbanite lives with the understanding that if it rains hard enough, the basement will occasionally take in a little water.

Hartman retired from the Police Department three years ago, when he turned 62. Except for one brief meeting on a downtown street, I had not seen him since he retired.

And now he had a story for me.

First, though, he caught me up on his life. He's still working as a custodian. He works a morning shift five days a week at the Mathews-Dickey Boys Club.

That's too far to walk, so he takes the bus. He catches that bus, Monday through Friday, at 6:30 in the morning. He makes, after taxes, $12.65 a day.

He doesn't really need the money. He gets a Social Security check and a pension from the city. Even without his job, he gets more than $700 a month.

He works to work, I suppose, but we didn't get into philosophy.

The Police Department owes him $4,822, he told me.

That's the figure Hartman came up with for his unused sick time. Knowing him, I'm sure it's accurate.

Under normal circumstances, I wouldn't look into a story like this. After all, Hartman retired more than three years ago. As a newspaperman, I have a statute of limitations floating around in my head. If something happened yesterday, fine. Last week or last month, maybe. Three years ago, forget it.

But I remembered how he used to come into the pressroom every night with his brush and his bucket, and I pictured him catching the bus every morning now. I figured that maybe just the thought of how he'd spend that $4,822 makes it easier to catch that early morning bus. Maybe he's been dreaming about going to Hawaii this winter.

So shortly after he left the newspaper, I went to the police station.

I was hoping, of course, that his paper work had gotten lost or mishandled, and I could sally in like a big shot reporter and get everything straightened out.

But life isn't a movie, and it turns out that back in 1986, the department didn't pay retirees for unused sick time.

In July of 1988, the department started paying retirees for 25 percent of their unused sick time, but that policy is not retroactive.

I went to the Railton to give Hartman the bad news.

I hope you weren't daydreaming about Hawaii, Grant, I said.

Oh no, he said. I was going to invest it. Maybe give some to my church, Christ in the City.

That made me feel a little better. Not getting money to invest or to give away, well, that's a disappointment, not a heartbreak.

You just retired too early, I said. You got a bad break.

Not my first, he said, and he said it matter-of-factly, without a trace of self-pity.

Wednesday, August 16, 1989.

He Leads Quiet Life as His
Home's Last Family Occupant

James O'Brien watches television these days, and he talks softly to his two dogs. Mostly, though, he remembers.

He is 87 years old, and what he remembers is the solitary life. He never married.

For a man who is comfortable with his memories, he lives in the perfect place.

"I could never leave this house," he told me.

This house is a brick house in a suburb north of St. Louis. It's an old house, but it dates from a time when things were built to last.

To O'Brien, it is a very special place.

His grandparents lived in the house. His parents lived in the house, and so did O'Brien and his only sibling, a sister.

At one time, the three generations shared the house. Years and years ago, the grandparents died, and then it was only two generations. Then the parents died, and O'Brien and his sister, who also never married, shared the house.

Seven years ago, his sister died.

I mentioned his sister in a column a few weeks ago. I was writing about a woman who does volunteer work at Baden school. She first volunteered when her youngest child was in kindergarten. The teacher, I wrote, was Gloria O'Brien, who had taught kindergarten for 44 years.

Shortly thereafter, I met a man who knows her brother. He told me about the house, how it had been occupied by the same family for three generations. Gloria's brother is the last of the line, the man said.

So I called the elderly bachelor, and arranged to visit. The house is clean — a college student comes in twice a day to care for the dogs and look after O'Brien — and O'Brien is alert.

He was an officer in a bank, and he was a bond clerk at a brokerage house. He worked at the brokerage house until he was 85 years old.

He never even came close to getting married.

"I used to weigh 230 pounds," he told me. "The girls were sensitive about it. They liked the slim guys."

O'Brien is 5 feet 8. He now weighs 125 pounds.

If the lack of a social life bothered him, it certainly wasn't apparent during my conversation with him.

"I was always a homebody," he said.

Indeed he was. He never traveled, never flew on an airplane, never left the state of Missouri. He received a draft notice during the Second World War, but he got a medical deferment because of a bad ear.

He knows the world, though, through his stamp collecting. He has approximately 500,000 stamps. He seldom looks at them anymore.

Stamp collecting was probably the perfect hobby for O'Brien. Collecting and saving things seems to run in the family.

After Gloria died, O'Brien's attorney, Jim McDowell, had the house cleaned. Six large dumpsters were needed. Gloria had saved everything that almost half a century's worth of kindergartners had made. There were boxes and boxes of papers.

The bedrooms were so jammed with papers that there was no place to sleep. Gloria slept on a couch. Her brother slept on a chair.

As I mentioned, the house is now clean. Most of the furniture is old. Almost by accident, O'Brien has collected antiques. Accumulated them, rather.

Much of the stuff belonged to his grandparents.

What was life like, I asked, during the years when he and his sister shared the old house together?

It was very comfortable, he said. The siblings were close, although Gloria, who was 12 years younger than her brother, was by far the more adventurous.

"She was a traveler," O'Brien said with a smile. "She took trips to Chicago, New York and Florida."

She didn't fly, either. She traveled by car with friends. Women friends.

"She didn't care too much for men," her brother said. "She had a good education. That's what she said, anyway."

Did she ever date, even as a younger woman?

"She went out with several young men," O'Brien said.

Was she ever close to marriage?

"I don't think so, but that would have been her business," O'Brien said.

He talked for a while about their life together. Some evenings she played the piano — she was a complete kindergarten teacher — while her brother studied his stamps.

She died at home during the heat wave of 1988.

Except for his dogs, O'Brien has been alone since.

Could I ask a very personal question? I inquired. He nodded.

If you had your life to live again, would you live it the same?

He paused for a moment to consider the question.

"I believe I would," he said.

With that, I left the house that is still, at least in memory, home to one man, two dogs and three generations.

Friday, April 7, 1995.

"They Used to Call Me the Beetle Bandit"

Edward "Stumpy" Gischer, who looks a lot older than his 54 years and is definitely not a testament to good living, went to the St. Louis County Courthouse on Wednesday morning to get a copy of his divorce. He needed it for some kind of dispute.

He walked through the metal detector, and the machine beeped.

"You got anything in your pockets? Empty your pockets, please," said Bob Colburn, one of the county cops who works security at the courthouse.

Gischer pulled assorted stuff out of his pockets — keys, a pack of smokes, a pipe — and handed it to Colburn, who looked closely at the pipe and sighed. It was the kind of pipe the dopers call a "one-hitter." That's because the bowl is just large enough for one good hit of pot.

"What's this?" asked Colburn.

Gischer looked at the pipe.

"It's not mine," he said.

Another sigh from Colburn, this one directed not so much at Gischer as at the entire human condition.

As the cops prepared to book Gischer for misdemeanor possession of drugs — there appeared to be a small amount of pot in the bowl of the pipe — Gischer asked the cops if they had ever heard of the "Beetle Bandit."

Nope, said the cops.

Gischer seemed a little disappointed.

"That's me," he said. "They used to call me the Beetle Bandit."

Indeed they did. He was one of the more clever guys ever to work in the local auto theft business. According to the old news stories, Gischer would buy old beat-up Volkswagens simply to get their titles and identification numbers.

Then he he would shift the identification numbers from those cars to stolen cars. During his heyday in the early '80s, Gischer was doing three cars a week.

Let me quote from one of those news stories.

"The scheme was notable not only for the number of cars involved, police say, but because of the cunning and craftsmanship brought to it."

The cunning part had to do with Gischer's penchant for Volkswagens. By sticking to the low end of the car market, he didn't draw much attention to himself. The craftsmanship had to do with transferring the identification numbers. One of the cops in the story called it a "super welding job."

Of course, this was in the arrest story. It's easy to be gracious when you've caught a guy.

The Beetle Bandit went to prison. He got out three years and a couple of heart attacks ago.

News of his bust Wednesday morning drifted around the courthouse and eventually reached Rich Koenig and Ken Tihen. They're investigators with the prosecuting attorney's office, but they used to be county cops. They remembered Gischer, and fondly, too. There is, after all, something of a bond between retired cops and the robbers they once chased.

"Stumpy was a thief with a good heart," said Tihen. "He just always thought it was easier to steal than to work."

I got Gischer's address off the booking sheet and stopped by his apartment Thursday morning. He lives in St. Louis on one of the streets named after a state.

"I'm the guy who was standing behind you in line

at the courthouse when you got busted yesterday," I said, by way of introduction. I also said I knew Tihen and Koenig.

"Good men, those two," he said. "Of course, I worked the other side of the street. Cat and mouse, you could say."

He talked wistfully about the old days. He said he had done some federal time for counterfeiting, and state time for burglary and, of course, auto theft. Only once did he ever go straight, he explained, and that was when he owned a bar for a couple of years. He said he won it in a dice game. Called it Stumpy's.

"The cops hated that I shut the place down," he told me. "They used to say it was handy because every thief in town used to hang out there. They never had to go looking for anybody."

The courthouse bust was a huge misunderstanding, he said. The jacket belonged to his daughter, who died recently. He didn't even check the pockets, he explained.

No big deal, I said. It's only a misdemeanor charge.

"I'm still on parole," he said.

He explained that his papers wouldn't be up until 2003. He said he didn't want to be revoked.

"I'm staying clean," he said. "I even go to church."

I looked at him. He's only 54, but he seemed old and frail. A little old man, 5 feet 2 inches and 130 pounds.

"With your health problems, it wouldn't make sense to put you back in prison," I said. "The prisons are overcrowded, anyway."

He shrugged.

"I don't know," he said. "They always seem to find a bed for me."

Friday, March 21, 1997.

His Needle Tracks Were
Path to Dead-End Life

The first cop at the scene did not recognize the man lying in the street. The man was clearly in bad shape. He had been shot in the head, in the chest and in the neck. He was wearing bib overalls and a Hawaiian-style shirt.

The cop glanced at the crowd that had already gathered. Even at 3 in the morning, a shooting draws a crowd. "Anybody got a name for this guy?" the cop asked.

Somebody did, and a bell sounded in the cop's mind. When the cop called the homicide department, he didn't use the standard, impersonal police jargon. He said, "Somebody just shot Marvin Allen."

Allen was still living, but barely, when the ambulance got there. A homicide sergeant rushed to Barnes Hospital in the unlikely event that Allen would regain consciousness long enough to make a statement.

"I know this guy," the sergeant said to the doctor.

Even as he said it, he noticed the needle tracks on one of Allen's arms.

The lieutenant who was running the district that night delivered the news to Allen's mother. That kind of assignment normally gets shucked off to a patrolman. Naturally, at that hour in the morning, Allen's mother was asleep when the doorbell rang. She hurried downstairs. News that comes in the middle of the night is never good news. She looked out the window and saw the lieutenant.

"I was hurt terribly when he told me," she said later, "but I can't say I was really surprised."

No, of course not. When your only son is leading a dead-end life, the cop at the door cannot be completely unexpected.

But there was another time, a different cop at the door. The news that night was similar, and yet totally different.

Detective Marvin Allen had been shot during a drug raid.

It was the night before Easter 11 years ago. The police department's elite Tactical Anti-Crime Team had learned, through an informant, that a large quantity of drugs was at a house on North Market but was going to be moved that night.

The detectives figured they had no time to get a search warrant. Instead, they decided to make a buy and then bust the place. The informant gave them the password, and the detectives went to the door.

Maybe the password had been changed. Maybe the drug dealers were nervous because they were about to move the drugs.

At any rate, the detectives gave the password and were answered by a hail of shots. Steve Jacobsmeyer, now a lieutenant, and Allen were hit. Jacobsmeyer caught a round in the neck that barely missed an artery. Allen was hit high on the right side of his chest.

Front-page news. Visits from top brass. Flowers from strangers.

To people who knew Allen, his status as a hero-cop was hardly surprising.

He grew up in the projects, but even as a kid he had lifted himself above his environment. While a lot of his playmates wound up in trouble as juveniles, Allen was a straight arrow. While his friends were dropping out of high school, Allen not only did well academically, he worked in a grocery store after school. He grew up without a father, but he quickly became the man of the family.

He fulfilled a dream when he joined the police department in 1970.

"He was a good cop, a hell of a policeman," said Steve Hobbs, the homicide sergeant who went to Barnes the night Allen died. "I'm not defending what he became later, but I worked with him in the Eighth District, and I know. He was good."

Allen's mother said her son especially liked helping kids in the projects.

Maybe that's because he came from the projects, maybe it's because he never got married, never had kids of his own. At any rate, he used to bring kids over to his mother's house. He organized games. He started a drum and bugle corps for the kids.

Allen's record indicates that he was, as Hobbs and others say, a hell of a policeman. He received two meritorious service citations and two letters of commendation. His assignment to an elite unit is further evidence of the regard in which he was held.

But at some point, and nobody really knows when, Allen started using drugs. His mother thinks it was after he was shot. She says he was in constant pain. Maybe that was it. Or maybe, during one of his countless investigations into the narcotics trade, he took a taste and started on his road down hill. As I say, nobody really knows.

We do know that he went on sick leave in May 1979 and, contrary to department rules, offered no evidence that he was seeing a doctor. His mother says he told her why he couldn't go to work.

"He didn't want to wear short sleeves," she says.

He didn't want his colleagues to see the needle tracks on his arms.

He resigned from the department in early July, and within two weeks he was arrested for attempted robbery. Ironically, the man he tried to rob was an off-duty cop.

He was also charged with two other robberies. He was convicted and sentenced to 20 years in prison. After an appeal, the sentence was amended to 15 years.

In a strange twist of fate, the drug dealer who had been convicted of shooting Jacobsmeyer and Allen later sued the two detectives. He contended that his rights had been violated.

By the time the case went to trial, Allen was in prison. He and the drug dealer were brought to court from Jefferson City in the same car.

The man lost his suit, by the way.

Allen was paroled in 1984, but his life never got back on track. He worked only sporadically. He was arrested once for possession of drugs. He was arrested once for drinking on a bus.

Jacobsmeyer ran into him a couple of years ago at a homicide scene at the Vaughn housing project. Allen was in the crowd of onlookers.

"I recognized him and went over to say hello. We talked for a couple of minutes, and he told me he was trying to get his life straightened out. But it was early in the morning, and he had a bottle in a brown paper bag," Jacobsmeyer recalls.

Allen's mother says her son was a proud man and was having a difficult time dealing with the failure his life had become.

"He had always been so good, so successful. And always, so nice. If you knew him when he was a little boy, you just wouldn't believe any of this now."

Monday, July 11, 1988.

Maybe Tulips Are All That's Certain

Under the rock-like surface the earth was moist and surprisingly soft. The hand-spade easily cut into the soil.

I gently placed the bulb in the earth and carefully covered it with dirt. Again and again I repeated the process.

Years ago I watched my father plant tulip bulbs in our backyard in Chicago. He handled the bulbs with uncharacteristic gentleness. With the naivete of youth, I thought him an unlikely gardener.

He was not a man who cared for flowers. If he ever bought my mother flowers, I was unaware of it. He was a rough man. He worked outside in the Chicago weather. He drank and he smoked, and he told wonderful stories in which police officers were always coppers and an arrest was always a pinch. He was a veteran of Guadalcanal. He told me he had been befriended by a head-hunter in New Guinea.

And yet he planted tulips.

As a child, and later as a young man, I couldn't understand the attraction my father seemed to have for tulips.

It has to do, I have finally realized, with the ability to protect things.

You plant the bulbs deep, several inches into the earth. If you plant them correctly, they are perfectly safe. A hard frost can't touch them. The bulbs wait out the long winter, and in the spring the flowers emerge from the ground.

Nothing else in life can be protected with such certainty.

For all his toughness, my father could not protect my sister from cancer. Nor could he protect my mother from her fatal illness.

As a person gets older, it is not just his own mortality he must confront. It is the absolute vulnerability of his friends and loved ones that comes into focus.

Here at the newspaper, which so often seems like the eye of the hurricane as we report on the misfortune of strangers, our own calm has been shattered in recent days. Not once, but twice.

First, Ann Kiburz was involved in a terrible accident. She remains in a coma, her prognosis uncertain.

Ann works in promotions. She is bright, and young, and beautiful, and she has always personified that overused cliche about being full of life.

On a recent and lovely afternoon, Ann and a friend drove to Hermann. Her friend was driving. I don't know the details of the accident — and to me, they hardly matter — but in the space of a moment the lives of two vibrant young women, and the lives of their families, were perhaps forever transformed.

On the heel of this dreadful news, Joe Pollack went to the hospital thinking he had a kidney stone. Instead, he had an abdominal aortic aneurism.

I understand very little about medicine, but according to the messages forwarded to the newspaper, his artery burst while he was at the hospital, and he was rushed into surgery.

He remains in very serious condition.

Two people I see nearly every day, two people I like and admire. Suddenly, both of them are fighting for their lives.

A car goes off the road, an artery bursts.

Life is, of course, a series of disasters. In the most fortunate of lives, much joy is interspersed with the disasters. But still, inevitably, the disasters come, and most often, they come with a shocking suddenness.

Friday night, as a friend and I drove down McCausland Avenue, we were stopped at a police roadblock.

"We just had a fatal accident," said the officer.

Sunday morning I read about it in the newspaper. Two cars collided at the intersection of McCausland and Dale. One of the cars spun around and struck a 26-year-old young man who was standing on the corner.

What the story didn't say — it consisted of just three sentences — was that it was a beautiful Friday night. A gorgeous Indian summer night.

A young man from the county had come into the city. He was standing at the corner, probably waiting to cross the street. Moments before, he'd probably been in one of the restaurants along McCausland, eating, talking with friends, waiting to pay the bill, doing something routine, while all along the two cars were winding along the city streets, like slow-motion comets hurtling toward each other.

The young man had no way of knowing.

So Saturday, and again Sunday, I picked up my handspade and went to the side of the house. I broke through the brittle surface and dug into the moist, soft earth.

As my father did years ago, I handled the bulbs with a gentleness that was really unnecessary. I carefully placed the bulbs into the earth. I covered them with several inches of soil. I then spread a layer of mulch over the entire bed.

They will be safe until spring, I said to myself.

As I surveyed my work, I realized why it is that the older a person gets, the more important gardening becomes.

Monday, October 31, 1994.

These Sounds of Love
Go Unheard, It Seems

The sounds of love — tapping, stamping, and small talk — hung in the air as the threesome moved along the sidewalk on the city's southwest side.

"How was school?" the middle-aged woman asked. "Good," said the 9-year-old girl. "How come Joey looks like a mummy?"

"We don't want him to get sick, so we bundle him up," said the woman. She stroked the blanket that covered the 11-month-old boy who was asleep in the baby-carrier that hung from the woman's shoulders.

Tap, tap, tap, went the woman's cane as the threesome moved off the sidewalk and into a street.

Stamp! went the little girl's foot as she stepped up on to a curb. The woman, recognizing the signal that a curb must be negotiated, stepped up.

Tapping, stamping, and making small talk, they continued their daily trek.

Doris Meyer is blind, but until this year, she never asked anybody for any favors.

She has worked all her adult life. For the past 24 years, she has been employed at Deaconess Hospital, where she is a medical transcriptionist, typing reports that doctors have dictated.

In 1981, she was certified as a foster parent. She asked for infants.

"I'd rather change them than chase them," she said.

The first child the state gave her was a 3-month-old girl named Shelli. The placement was supposed to be temporary, but Shelli never left. Four and a half years later, Meyer adopted the child.

She enrolled her daughter in one of the city's magnet schools.

Each morning, a neighbor who was driving her child to a Catholic school would drop Shelli off at Dewey School, where Shelli would board the school bus that took her to the magnet school.

Each afternoon, when the parents of another magnet school student picked up their child at Dewey, they'd give Shelli a lift home.

But this year, those parents no longer pick up their child, and that means Shelli, now 9 years old, is dropped off alone, six blocks from her home at McCausland and Nashville avenues.

As far as Meyer is concerned, six blocks is too far for a 9-year-old girl to travel alone, especially in the winter when the sun is already setting when the bus arrives at the vacant Dewey school.

So every day, Meyer makes the six-block trek to meet the bus.

For a good part of the walk, the sidewalks are chipped and broken. Even with a cane, it's impossible for Meyer to make the walk without an occasional stumble.

Then there are the dogs. Meyer knows from experience that a cane seems to arouse dogs. Usually, the dogs are behind fences, but Meyer can't see the dogs, can't see the fences, and when the barking starts, she always feels a flash of fear.

Compounding the problem is the fact Meyer most often is traveling with an infant.

Shelli was her first foster child, but far from her last. The baby she has right now is her 21st. For the most part, Meyer is given babies who have been abused or neglected.

In case you're wondering how Meyer can work full-time and still care for a baby, she hires a baby sitter.

Her monthly cost for a sitter is higher than the stipend the state pays her. Obviously, money doesn't have anything to do with Meyer's decision to be a foster parent.

"I feel like I'm doing something positive. Besides, Shelli and I like having a baby around," Meyer said. "One night, when Shelli was saying her prayers, she said, 'Please, Jesus, send all our babies back to us.' I said, 'Please, Jesus, not all at once.' "

Meyer realized it would be difficult, maybe impossible, to care for a baby this winter if she were forced to carry that baby six blocks in bad weather, over sidewalks that are difficult enough even when not covered with snow or ice.

So shortly before school started, she wrote a letter to the head of transportation for the city's board of education.

"I am not asking you to cab her, or even change the bus route. All I ask is that you put a morning and afternoon stop on the southeast corner of McCausland and Nashville," she wrote.

When the official didn't respond, Meyer called him on the phone. He said that just because the bus went down McCausland in the past did not mean it would go down McCausland in the future.

"Sure enough, this year they changed the route," said Meyer.

So she wrote a letter to each member of the school board.

Not a single member responded.

Last month, Meyer got a letter from Governor John Ashcroft in which the governor praised her for participation in the foster care program.

She wrote the governor and explained her predicament.

Shortly thereafter, she received a note from the governor's office. The note said her letter had been turned over to the commissioner of the Department of Elementary and Secondary Education for review.

That was a month ago.

As for now, you can still see the threesome slowly moving along in the fading light. You can hear them, too.

Tapping, stamping and making small talk.

Wednesday, November 22, 1989.

Love and Tragedy Are Intertwined

Dan Hammer grew up in St. Louis and moved to Houston several years ago. There he met Jeanine.

They fell in love and got married. They lived in an apartment, and spent many nights listening to Bruce Springsteen records. They especially liked an album called "The River." Like most of Springsteen's material, the songs are about regular people, and love, and broken dreams. Love and sadness, forever intertwined.

There was much love but little sadness in the lives of Dan and Jeanine. They had a daughter, and then, at Dan's urging, they moved to St. Louis. Dan knew first-hand that this is a fine place to raise children.

Life was good when they moved back here. Dan came from a large, loving family, and it was nice to be surrounded by that love. Jeanine, who was a nurse, found a good job in a doctor's office. Dan found a good job, too.

They bought a house, nice but not fancy, in a neighborhood that can best be described as solid middle class. The house was within walking distance of the parish school.

That meant a lot to Dan.

So there they were, living in their first house, caring for their first child. Like countless other young couples, they were ready to march quietly into the future.

Regular readers of this column know what happened next. Jeanine became ill. The diagnosis was terrible — inoperable cancer. She went into the hospital for two weeks of treatment, and Dan stayed with her.

When he went back to work, he discovered that his boss, a fundamentalist Christian, had hired someone to replace him.

That was in May.

I wrote a column about the Christian boss. He told me that he was praying for Jeanine, but business is business, and if a guy's wife has terminal cancer, there's no telling when he'll have to miss work.

In a sense, the Christian boss did Dan and his family a favor. At a time like that, it was nice to have a villain. It felt good to be able to direct anger at somebody. After all, the real nightmare was the cancer, and who can you blame for that?

That was in May.

After I wrote the column, I had only one occasion to talk to Dan. A fellow called me and said he might be interested in hiring Dan. I took the man's phone number and called Dan. Jeanine answered.

How are you feeling? I asked.

Pretty good, all things considered, she said.

Then Dan came on the phone, and I gave him the man's number. Then I wished him well and suggested, lamely, that we stay in touch.

Jeanine died this summer. I saw the notice on the obituary page.

I thought briefly about going to the funeral, but decided not to. That was because this story had touched me in a way that most stories don't.

Like most newspaper reporters, I often write about terrible things. After all, much of news has to do with ordinary people thrown into tragic circumstances.

Still, there was something about this story that really struck home. Maybe it had to do with the fact that Dan and Jeanine seemed so nice, so ordinary. Maybe I was touched because their daughter is just a year younger than mine.

Or maybe it had to do with something else. The

kind of tragedy I'm accustomed to writing about is violent in nature. Before I became a columnist, I wrote about crime, about murder.

But somehow murder seems like news, and cancer doesn't. Had Dan's boss not fired him, I wouldn't have written about Dan's situation. In fact, had Dan's boss not been a fundamentalist Christian, I wouldn't have written anything. That was the news peg — Christian does un-Christianlike thing.

Broken dreams were just a sidelight. Love and sadness, forever intertwined. I leave that stuff to songwriters.

Earlier this week, I saw Dan's name on the obituary page. He was 28 years old.

He died of a broken heart, although the official cause of death is listed as carbon monoxide poisoning.

Dan's death was hard to take. This time, there was nobody to get angry at, no made-to-order villain. Just an illness called depression, and whom can you blame for that?

I know Dan loved his daughter, and one of the ironies of the whole thing is that Dan knew his large and loving family would take care of the child. To do what he did, he had to be sure of that.

Love and sadness, forever intertwined.

One of Dan's sisters, a young woman with three children and a fourth on the way, is going to adopt the little girl. She'll grow up surrounded by love.

What Dan did is, of course, irrational, and it would be wrong to draw any moral lessons from an irrational act. Nevertheless, when I think about the whole story, one lesson comes to mind.

If you're lucky enough to love somebody, appreciate what you have.

Friday, September 16, 1988.

Lieutenant Knows His Place
with Platoon Sergeant

Sgt. Ervin Emrick was 29 years old when Paul Ebaugh met him in December 1968, but it was an old 29. Emrick was a platoon sergeant. He was on his third tour in Vietnam. He knew the secrets of life.

Ebaugh was five years younger. He was, at least in theory, supposed to be Emrick's boss. He was a lieutenant.

He had just arrived in-country. He was choppered out to the bush to join Kilo Company of the Third Battalion, Fifth Marine Regiment. The company had been in the field for more than a month participating in a meat-grinder of an operation called Mead River. It was late in the afternoon when Ebaugh joined the company. He was to take command of the second platoon.

Another lieutenant greeted him, and then introduced him to Emrick, the man who was really in charge of the second platoon. Emrick took Ebaugh over to the platoon's position. As they walked, Emrick glanced at his new lieutenant.

"If you want to live very long out here, lieutenant, you'll take those blanking bars off your shoulders," he said, although his language was not quite so delicate.

Ebaugh, who was smart enough to know how little he knew, took the bars off.

That night it rained — for which Ebaugh would be eternally grateful — and as he and Emrick huddled under a poncho, Emrick asked him where he was from.

"Missouri," said the new lieutenant.

"What part of Missouri?" asked the staff sergeant.

"Southeast Missouri," said Ebaugh.

"What part of southeast Missouri?" asked Emrick.

"Cape Girardeau," said Ebaugh.

"Where in Cape Girardeau?" asked Emrick.

Emrick, too, had been raised in Cape Girardeau. The two men had not known each other back home. Maybe that was because of the age difference. Five years is practically a generation gap when you're in school. Maybe part of it had to do with the different life tracks they were on. Ebaugh was one of those kids who were always headed for college. Emrick was one of those guys who never seemed headed anywhere in particular — until he joined the Marine Corps.

On his first tour in Vietnam, he caught rheumatic fever and was offered a medical discharge. He refused. He was badly wounded during his second tour, and when he recovered from his wounds, he was offered embassy duty, recruitment duty or assignment as a drill instructor. Instead, he chose to go back to Vietnam. He was wounded again but was back in the bush by the time Ebaugh arrived.

At 29, Emrick was unmarried. If the Marine Corps wanted you to have a wife, they'd issue you one.

If Ebaugh had any doubt that Emrick was the genuine article, those doubts were erased on that first day after the rainy night. The platoon slogged through a ville, and after a defensive perimeter was set up, Ebaugh, Emrick, the radioman, and a forward observer sat down for lunch.

Ebaugh put his hand on the ground and leaned back. Leaned way back! His hand had slipped into a hole and his body twisted around. He found himself looking into the hole. He was staring at a grenade.

It was a common booby trap, a toe-popper. The enemy had dug a hole, fiddled with the grenade so it would go off without a delay, attached a trip wire to the pin on the grenade, placed a piece of cardboard over the hole and then covered the cardboard with some dirt.

When someone stepped on the cardboard, the trip wire would pull the pin. Fortunately for Ebaugh, the previous night's rain had soaked the cardboard and his hand went through the cardboard without yanking the trip wire.

Ebaugh froze. The radioman and forward observer pulled back. But Emrick, quick as a cat, had his hand in the hole, holding the pin in place.

"Back off real easy now, lieutenant," he said.

Things went like that for the next few weeks. Emrick taught the lieutenant how to survive and how to lead men in combat.

By May, Emrick was with another platoon in the company, but the two men stayed close.

In the second week of May, the company was plodding through rice paddies when a heavily dug-in contingent of NVA opened fire from a tree line. Twenty-two Marines were killed that day. One of them was Emrick. He was shot when he left his cover to try to reach a wounded Marine.

The lieutenant he had tutored wrote the commendation papers for the Silver Star that was awarded posthumously.

Ebaugh is now a successful businessman with a wife and two grown daughters. He'll be 52 in August.

Emrick, of course, will always be 29.

There's a small memorial dedicated to him in Cape Girardeau. It's in a park by the river. If you see a middle-aged man visiting that memorial sometime during this Fourth of July weekend, leave him to his own thoughts. He's a private man, and he seldom talks about the war. He used to be a lieutenant.

Friday, July 5, 1996.

What Would Grizzard Think?

Atlanta — Looking for the Ghost of Lewis Grizzard . . .

The American South, at once fiercely proud and bitterly ashamed of its past, is a place of ghosts, and the one I most wanted to contact was that of Lewis Grizzard, who died in March of 1994.

He used to be a newspaper columnist here in Atlanta.

In truth, he was a bit more than a newspaper columnist. He was a real Southern writer - although he hated the label, and would sometimes wonder why he was called a Southern writer and Mike Royko was never called a Midwestern writer.

Maybe that's because there is a certain feel to the South, an attitude, away of speaking, and Grizzard was in touch with every bit of it.

I remember a story about a man who was drinking at a place called Slick's Lounge. Two other fellows started arguing, things got out of hand, one of the fellows pulled a gun, shot and missed his tormentor, but hit the first fellow, the innocent bystander, in the knee.

Grizzard quoted the victim: "Man, I was just sittin' there drinkin' a Schlitz, and some fool shot my ass in the knee."

That's good Southern writing.

Grizzard - and that's Grizzard, rhymes with lard - loved the South, and he especially loved Atlanta and his native state of Georgia. As I wandered around Atlanta these last few days, I started wondering what Grizzard would think about these Olympic Games.

Not much, I figured. He would positively hate the way the Yankees and the foreigners are criticizing the place. The local paper continues to run a piece called "As Others See Us" each day, and as the headline over Wednesday's installment said, "The Furor Grows."

Sadly, Grizzard did not have the self-depreciating humor of a Jeff Foxworthy, the self-proclaimed redneck comedian. In a comedy routine he has done about these Atlanta Games, he imagines what the events would be like if the locals had really been able to organize them. He has the discus throwers tossing Ford hubcaps, and he envisions the hammer toss. First, you pick up the hammer, he says. "Hit your thumb as hard as you can and then chuck it," he says. "If you don't cuss, it don't count."

Would Grizzard have been amused?

Furthermore, I doubt that Grizzard would have liked the Games themselves. Sportswise, he could have been from Texas. He loved football. To think that these Games have everything from ping pong to ballroom dancing, but no football, would have left him bumfuzzled.

That's a Southern word. Grizzard used it a lot. It doesn't translate well into real English. Perplexed is pretty close.

At any rate, I decided to go ghost-chasing. First, I went to a bookstore in downtown Atlanta. Knowing that Grizzard had published a number of books of his columns, I asked the young man at the counter where they kept the Grizzard books.

"Who?" asked the young man.

An older woman who had overheard my question immediately interceded and led me to what seemed to be an entire shelf of Grizzard books. I selected "Chili Dawgs Always Bark at Night" and "Don't Bend Over in the Garden, Granny, You Know Them Taters Got Eyes."

I took them back to the Olympic Press Center near Centennial Park, and while my colleagues from a hundred different countries watched the Games on countless television sets - more trouble with the shuttle buses, apparently -I immersed myself in the considerable wit and questionable wisdom of a fine Southern writer.

Questionable wisdom, I say, because the truth is, I don't buy into a lot of Grizzard's philosophy. He was pretty much of a confirmed sexist. Maybe that's what four wives will do to a guy.

Incidentally, Grizzard was so big around here that his third wife, after their divorce, actually wrote her own book. It was titled, "How to Tame a Wild Bore."

When Grizzard was asked about it, he was uncharacteristically chivalrous.

"I'd say it was the best book any of my ex-wives have ever written," he said.

Back to his questionable wisdom. He was pretty much a Republican. Maybe that's what 12 books and three comedy albums will do to a guy. He probably thought a lot about taxes.

At any rate, I looked through the books for some clue as to what Grizzard would think of the Olympics. There was only one column about any of the Olympic sports, and the column was titled, "Why I Get No Kick Out of Soccer."

Like so many Americans with no children, Grizzard had never learned to appreciate soccer. He wrote, "If soccer were an American soft drink, it would be Diet Pepsi."

Unless you've spent some time in Atlanta, you can't

understand what a serious insult that is. This is Coca Cola City. In fact, the big joke going around in these Games is this: "Did you hear the Chinese swimmers tested positive for Pepsi?"

Still, that's all I got out of the books. Grizzard did not like soccer. I continued my research by calling Ron Hudspeth, who was one of Grizzard's best friends and steadiest drinking mates, which were, for Grizzard, pretty much the same thing.

Hudspeth used to write a column for the local paper. Eventually, he found honest work and now publishes "The Hudspeth Report," which chronicles Atlanta nightlife.

"Lewis would not have liked the Olympics," Hudspeth told me.

I asked how best to chase his ghost.

Hudspeth thought for a moment. The singles bar that Grizzard loved the most, Harrison's on Peach tree, closed a few years ago, Hudspeth said. He suggested I try the country club where Grizzard spent a lot of time.

"He used to have a routine. He'd start out with a screwdriver. Then he'd have vodka with just a splash of orange juice. Then he'd have a double vodka with a splash of orange juice," Hudspeth said.

If the country club wasn't my style, I should check out Manuel's Tavern, Hudspeth said. I grabbed a cab.

Manuel's Tavern brings to mind O'Connell's Pub in St. Louis. Good drinks, good hamburgers, casual atmosphere.

In his early days on the newspaper, Grizzard had spent a lot of time there, Hudspeth had told me. Then there had been some kind of a falling out between Grizzard and Manuel Maloof, the tavern's owner.

Some stories had it that Grizzard wanted Manuel to close the tavern for a book-signing of his "KathySue Loudermilk, I Love You" but that Manuel refused. At any rate, Grizzard quit being a regular.

Maloof, who is now 72 years old, was sitting at a table in the corner when I arrived. He denied the stories about a falling-out.

"He became 'Gucci' Grizzard. That's what happened," Manuel told me. "He used to be a redneck. He'd stand up at the bar there and drink long-neck Pabst Blue Ribbon almost every day. Then he made a lot of money and moved to Buckhead. I don't know anything about a book-signing. We have book-signings here all the time."

Manuel also said that he liked Grizzard personally but did not like the stuff he wrote.

"I'm a Democrat. I'm an old-fashioned liberal. I come from the time of Franklin Delano Roosevelt," he said. "But personally, I liked Grizzard. Don't get that wrong."

Back at my bar stool, I met Scotty Polinsky, who had stopped in for a drink. He used to tend bar at The Bucket Shop in the old Underground Atlanta complex. That was another of Grizzard's haunts.

"He'd have thought the Olympics was a farce," Polinsky told me. "We all do."

A dissenting vote came from Bill McCloskey, who has worked at Manuel's for 22 years.

"He wouldn't have liked the crowds, and he'd have made fun of the whole thing, but deep down, I think he would have enjoyed it," McCloskey said.

A little later, I spoke with another bartender, Bobby Agee.

"Grizzard was a little strange," Agee said. "I remember making him a drinkin a glass like this," he said, showing me a normal cocktail glass, "and he took the drink and poured it into a plastic cup. And he wasn't leaving. He just wanted it in the plastic cup."

That certainly is strange, and for the first time, I felt like I might be making contact. Anyone who prefers his liquor in a plastic cup might like these Olympic Games. You have some very fine athletic competition in the midst of some tacky surroundings. Good booze in plastic cups.

Still, I don't know. I saw a little item in the Regional Roundup of the Atlanta paper. Two men were having an early-morning Bible-quoting contest. The fellow who lost got angry and shot and killed the man who had known more Scripture.

I like to think that that's the story Grizzard would have gone after, but that stuff about the plastic cup has me bumfuzzled.

Thursday, July 25, 1996.

Brinks Job Was on
the Money, Ex-robber Says

Joe Smith was a bank robber back in the days when robbing banks was a high-status crime.

"Yeah, we'd case the bank, and we'd plan the job, and we'd be after a lot of money. Not the way they do it today," he said.

The way they do it today is very low-rent. A guy walks in, hands the teller a note and a bag and then runs out after the teller puts some money in the bag. Often, the guy doesn't even have a gun.

Almost always, these low-rent bank robbers get caught.

That's not to say that Smith was entirely successful. In fact, he spent 24 years in prison.

He got out several years ago and is now a mid-level executive for a small company in St. Louis. Many of the people he deals with don't know his background, which is why I am not using his real name.

I visited him at his office a couple of days ago. I wondered if he had been following the news - rather, the lack of news - about the $900,000 robbery of an armored car guard in St. Louis several weeks ago.

It was, it seems, the perfect crime. Nobody was hurt, and the robbers got away with almost a million dollars in unmarked cash.

Two robbers, wearing white overalls and masks, surprised the guard in the basement hallway of the Equitable Building as he was wheeling a cart containing more than $1 million from the United Missouri Bank to the Brinks truck outside.

The robbers bound the guard with tape, locked him in the storeroom and escaped with five money bags. Later, the overalls and $1,000 in $1 bills were discovered on the vacant 13th floor.

"You read about it?" I asked Smith.

"Every word," he said. "It's nice to know there are still some professionals out there."

Smith, by the way, is contemptuous of today's criminal element.

I asked if he had ever thought of doing an armored car.

"It used to be one of my fantasies," he said. "I was in Leavenworth with some guys who did a Brinks job. It was way, way above bank robberies. You had to have all of your facts together."

He quickly added that although such a job had once been a fantasy of his, he had had nothing to do with this one.

Frankly, this was the kind of job that could have been anybody's fantasy, I said.

"Bingo," he said.

What do you mean? I asked.

"I wouldn't be surprised if the guys who did it are at work today in that building, wearing suits and looking normal," he said.

How so? I asked.

"This was an inside job. Somebody had been watching the guards and knew where they'd be and when they'd be there. More importantly, somebody knew the 13th floor was vacant. That makes me think it was somebody who works in that building."

You mean a businessman?

"Sure. Of course, they could have had somebody do it for them. Some friends from out of town, or something."

You mean, it would be like if I suddenly realized that there was a million dollars for the taking, and maybe I'd call some old buddies from the service?

"That's how these things work," Smith said. "You

see a score, and you call some old friends from prison, or, like you say, maybe some buddies from the service. But in this instance, I've got a feeling that the guys who did it aren't from prison. If they ever catch them, I think they're going to find out that the guys don't have rap sheets. That's just a feeling I've got."

So you think it was businessmen.

"There's another possibility - cops."

Cops?

"Don't kid yourself. If the guys didn't work in the building, it had to be somebody with a lot of information. Cops have a lot of information. Along those lines, you also have to think about the guards."

The FBI says the guards have been cleared, I said.

Smith shrugged.

"The guards are the most obvious, so I'm sure they gave them a long look," he said.

I asked Smith what could trip the guys up now. Maybe they'd start spending the money foolishly.

"I've got an idea these are guys who know how to spend money," he said.

Maybe loose talk then. If I pulled off the perfect crime, it would be hard not to tell somebody about it, I said.

Smith shook his head.

"No, no, no. You don't understand. This is something inside you. You do something like this for yourself."

Although the answer was already obvious, I asked Smith if he hopes the robbers eventually get caught.

"Nope," he said with a grin. "Look, if you're an actor and you do a great job, you win an Oscar. If you're a criminal, and you do a great job, all you can get is away."

Monday, December 7, 1992.

How Bus Rider Gets Stuck with a Suit

oe Bates wants to become a physicist. Other than that, he is a normal 18-year-old kid.

He graduated from Southwest High School in June. He didn't have a car, so he had to rely on public transportation to get to school. Every morning, he rode a Bi-State bus to school, and every afternoon, he rode a Bi-State bus home.

When Joe starts at the University of Missouri at St. Louis this fall, he expects to be riding the bus.

In short, Joe is the kind of faithful rider that Bi-State ought to be nice to. Maybe the Bi-State bosses ought to invite Joe into their corporate offices so he could do his homework in comfortable surroundings. After all, the bosses are spending $500,000 to remodel.

At the very least, Bi-State ought to leave Joe alone.

His problems really began eight months ago. As he did every afternoon after school, he caught a bus on Kingshighway and rode it south to Oakland. There he planned to transfer to a bus that would travel west on Oakland.

He was lucky, or so it seemed. As he hopped off the first bus, he saw the second bus. He ran across the street to board it.

He leaped onto the steps leading to the front door. He was halfway in the bus when the door closed, and the bus headed west on Oakland.

The bus did not go very far before the driver noticed that there was something amiss. That something was Joe. His right arm and his right leg were inside the bus. The rest of Joe was outside.

So the driver stopped the bus, and the rest of Joe clambered aboard.

We all know what kind of a litigious society this is,

and Bi-State is a favorite target. I remember a case in 1979 in which a bus was involved in an accident. After the bus stopped, spectators overpowered the driver and climbed aboard so they could claim to have been injured.

Frankly, lawsuits have been filed for far less cause than what happened to Joe. So it's not surprising that Joe and Bi-State are embroiled in a lawsuit.

What is surprising is this: Bi-State is suing Joe.

Technically, Bi-State has named Joe as a third-party defendant, and has alleged that he is responsible for getting stuck halfway in the bus.

You see, when the bus came to a sudden stop to let Joe get unstuck, a woman was injured.

She subsequently sued Bi-State, and her lawsuit alleges that she was "severely and permanently injured in that plaintiff's head, neck, back, arms, legs and all of the muscles and soft tissues therefore were severely and seriously bruised, contused, lacerated, cut, torn, stretched, aggravated, ruptured, mashed, wrenched, compressed, abraded, dislocated, sprained and strained."

In addition, the woman's nervous system has been ruined and she has suffered a lot of mental anguish, the suit contends. Furthermore, it says, her injuries are "permanent and progressive."

The woman is asking for $50,000.

As lawsuits go, that's not a lot of money, so I figured that maybe her attorney was overstating her injuries. The attorney's name is Michael Gunn, and I called him and asked if he could describe - in layman's terms - the injuries his client had suffered.

"She had a broken tooth," he said.

Gunn also explained that his client had indeed been bruised, and that she had suffered a great deal of pain.

Maybe she deserves $50,000. That's up to a judge and a jury to decide, and I have no opinion on the matter.

But it certainly seems ludicrous that Bi-State is suing Joe. After all, it ought to be the bus driver's responsibility to make sure that no one is stuck in the door when the bus starts rolling. That seems like an elementary precaution.

I called the attorney who is handling the case for Bi-State. His name is Daniel Rabbitt. He explained that if Joe had not been stuck in the door, the bus wouldn't have had to come to a sudden stop. Therefore, the whole thing is Joe's fault.

I agreed that the bus wouldn't have been forced to stop if Joe hadn't been stuck, but it doesn't necessarily follow that it's Joe's fault that the driver closed the door on him. In fact, it seems unfair.

Rabbitt explained that Joe was not facing any financial hardship no matter how the lawsuit turns out. His parents have insurance, and Joe is covered by their policy.

He has insurance, so why not sue him? That's not the kind of reasoning you'd expect from Bi-State. I wonder if any Bi-State executives were among the crowd that jumped on the bus after the accident in 1979.

Friday, July 18, 1986.

Man of the Road Rings in Christmas

The bell ringer was home from his job, if you can call it home, if you can call it a job.

He's staying at the Harbor Light Mission on Washington Avenue. He's making $3.35 an hour ringing the bells at a Salvation Army collection point. Wednesday was his first day on the job. He worked at a National Food Store in High Ridge. He's probably working someplace else today. The Salvation Army likes to move its people around. The bell ringer hopes to get five or six days' work in before he heads out of town. Maybe he'll sell a little blood on the way out, build up the cash reserves before heading south toward warmer weather.

He'd like to be in Texas or California by Christmas. He calls himself a road man.

The term hobo, which is what you or I might call the bell ringer, is not used anymore. It makes you think of men riding the rails. That doesn't happen much these days. Don Diercks, who runs the Harbor Light, remembers when transients routinely inquired about the rail yards. The subject doesn't come up anymore.

Today's version of the hobo goes by bus when he's flush. He hitchhikes when he's not.

The bell ringer plans to take the Greyhound to Joplin. Then he'll ride his thumb and thereby keep a nice cash reserve.

Of course, all plans are subject to change. That's especially true for a road man. There's a certain freedom in not knowing what you'll do next.

"If I want to see the ocean, I go," the bell ringer says. "Look at you. You probably have a family and a house, and I know you got a job. You couldn't just leave if you wanted to."

We're having coffee in the canteen at the Harbor Light. This is the second time I've met the bell ringer. He is not at all what I expected when I first talked to Diercks about drifters leaving St. Louis for warmer weather.

The bell ringer, who is 42 years old, is somehow less ravaged than I expected.

He checked into the Harbor Light's detoxification unit a couple of days ago, but he doesn't seem like a skid-row type.

He isn't, he assures me. He explains that a road man has to know how to play the angles, and the best angle in this case was the detox. Three nights in a bed, good meals, and then a chance to be a bell ringer and pick up some cash. Had he checked in as a transient, there would have been no bed. He'd be sleeping on the floor and going to soup kitchens for his meals, he says.

This is true, I later find out.

"I lucked into this," the bell ringer says. "This was stone luck that there was room in detox. I've been here once before, and I knew that detox was the route to try."

The bell ringer says he's been on the road for 1 year. He says he has 20 more to go.

Would you take a decent job if you could find one, I ask.

Sure, for a week, he replies.

He talks philosophically about the freedom of the road. He doesn't own a thing, he says, and he never will. He does what he wants, and he goes where he wants. He has nothing to be ashamed of.

Then why the request not to use his name?

He has a 21-year-old son, he says, and he wouldn't want his boy to read about him.

Why not, if life on the road is so good?

The bell ringer shrugs. It's a hard life, and he doesn't think his son could handle it. Not many can. You couldn't, he says.

Sometimes he's three days without a meal. Then, too, there's an occasional trip to jail. The longest stretch he ever did was 1 day in Columbus, Ind., for being a public nuisance.

He says he doesn't have any friends. There are very few true road men around. Not many people are homeless by choice.

"Don't get me wrong. I'm not putting myself above anybody, but I see a lot of losers," the bell ringer says.

It must get lonely.

"The only person I got is me," the bell ringer says. "I'm married to myself. That's the way I look at it."

He deflects a question about his family. "That was over a long time ago," he says. "I don't feel close to anybody."

The bell ringer shrugs again at the mention of Christmas.

"I'll probably be on the road," he says. "Nine times out of 10, I'll be on the road. I don't feel in my heart that I have any place to go."

I thank the bell ringer for his time, and he heads back into the dormitory, which he is sharing, temporarily, with a bunch of men he doesn't know.

I head home, toward my wife and daughter.

Who cares about seeing the ocean?

Friday, December 6, 1985.

Christmastime's Magical
Moments Wrapped in Love

Many many years ago, in a city far to our north, there lived a family with seven children. Marjorie was the oldest.

If you had to describe the family's economic situation, you would call it middle class. Maybe even lower middle class. But whatever it was, it was comfortable and secure. At least it seemed so to the children.

Truth is, there were storm clouds just over the horizon. The most personal had to do with the health of the father. As a child, he had suffered from rheumatic fever. The illness had left him with a weakened heart.

But the children were unaware of their father's health problem. More precisely, they were unaware of its implications. The fact that their father was not a robust man - you and I might call him sickly - was just that, a fact. Neither good nor bad. Just a fact.

Oddly enough, the children recall their father as a man of extraordinary strength. His strength was spiritual rather than physical. He was a man of great religious faith. It was not the type of faith that manifests itself in self-righteousness. His God was a loving God.

The house and the family were filled with love.

Because of the father's religious faith, the holiday season was not festive. The father believed in Advent. That is, the weeks before Christmas were spent in quiet contemplation. Like a true Christian, he was preparing himself for the celebration of the birth of Jesus.

The children, on the other hand, were waiting for Christmas Eve.

They knew that their father had already bought a Christmas tree and had stored it in the garage. They knew that at precisely 6:30 on Christmas Eve, their parents would send them upstairs to bed. Then their parents would bring in the Christmas tree, decorate it and put the presents underneath it.

Sometime after 11, their parents would leave the house to go to midnight Mass.

Technically, of course, their father - their devout father! - was rushing the end of Advent by a few hours. But as I've said, his God was a loving God and therefore understood that seven children would wake up early on Christmas morning and expect to find a well-decorated Christmas tree.

At any rate, there was a magical moment to all of this.

And that magical moment came when the children had been sent upstairs and their father brought the tree in from the garage.

When the tree was brought from the cold garage into the warm house, an overpowering scent of pine wafted upstairs. It filled the nostrils of the children. For them, this sudden smell of pine meant Christmas.

The oldest boy was always detailed to hide near the top of the stairs and to report to the rest of the children when their parents had left for church.

Then the children would tumble down the stairs, gaze in wonderment at the tree and the presents and finally rush upstairs as their parents returned from church.

And so it went, year after year, even as the storm clouds gathered over the horizon.

The father's heart grew ever weaker. On a grander scale, an unemployed house painter was gaining a following in Germany.

Eventually, the storms came. The father died at the age of 47, while the youngest children were still children. The oldest son, the boy who had once hid near the top of the stairs, was killed in World War II.

On his very last bombing mission - he was scheduled to come home after the flight - his plane was hit and he bailed out over the English Channel. His body was never recovered.

By this time, Marjorie was a Dominican nun. Eventually, three of her four sisters joined her in the order.

Marjorie is now 70 years old. She is happy, and at peace, but every year as Christmas approaches, she follows the same ritual.

First, she buys a small tree. But that is not enough. So then she buys pineboughs and scatters them around her small apartment. But that is not enough.

Finally, then, she buys an aerosol can of pine scent. She sprays it, almost madly, around the apartment. She breathes in the odor.

For an instant, as the scent of pine overwhelms her, she catapults back in time.

One of her younger sisters, a nun here in St. Louis, is a friend of mine. She lovingly kids Marjorie about the ritual.

But also, she understands.

That sudden rush of pine scent can throw her, too, back to a simpler time when the family was whole and Christmas had a magic that went beyond even religion.

Enjoy what you have this holiday season, my friend

tells me, and I pass the message on to you on this Christmas Eve.

If you're blessed enough to be surrounded by love, rejoice.

Friday, December 24, 1993.

ABOUT THE AUTHOR

A native of Chicago, Bill McClellan began a checkered-collegiate career with an unsuccessful stint at University of Illinois. That led to the loss of his student deferment and a hitch in the Marine Corps. Afterwards, he attended Arizona State University.

He worked on the Phoenix Gazette before coming to St. Louis in 1980.

His first book, *Evidence of Murder*, documented the case of Edward Post, a New Orleans businessman who was convicted of killing his wife at a real estate convention in St. Louis.

McClellan and his wife, Mary, have two children, Lorna and Jack.

*"Grinning & Baring an Intrepid Dad's Life
on the Skids ... the dog, and readers,
get the last laugh!"*